For my dad

Networked

A Contemporary History of News in Transition

Adrienne Russell

polity

First published in 2011 by Polity Press

Polity Press
65 Bridge Street
Cambridge CB2 1UR, UK

Polity Press
350 Main Street
Malden, MA 02148, USA

ISBN-13: 978-0-7456-4951-1
ISBN-13: 978-0-7456-4952-8(pb)

A catalogue record for this book is available from the British Library.

Typeset in 11 on 13 pt Adobe Sabon
by Servis Filmsetting Ltd, Stockport, Cheshire
Printed and bound in Great Britain by MPG Books Group Limited, Bodmin, Cornwall

The publisher has used its best endeavours to ensure that the URLs for external websites referred to in this book are correct and active at the time of going to press. However, the publisher has no responsibility for the websites and can make no guarantee that a site will remain live or that the content is or will remain appropriate.

Every effort has been made to trace all copyright holders, but if any have been inadvertently overlooked the publisher will be pleased to include any necessary credits in any subsequent reprint or edition.

For further information on Polity, visit our website: www.politybooks.com

Contents

Acknowledgements

Thanks to the Annenberg Center for Communication at the University of Southern California for time and funds and for the inspiration I drew from my colleagues there as the ideas of this book were coming together. Thanks to the American University of Paris and to the University of Denver for providing the rich personal and academic environments in which I undertook this project and for the time and money that were essential for me to get things done. And thanks to my colleagues at the University of Denver's Digital Media Studies Program who have deepened my understanding of technology and culture in ways that have greatly influenced this book.

Thanks also to my editors at Polity, Andrea Drugan and Lauren Mulholland, who are great at what they do, and to the anonymous reviewers of the first, very rough draft of the book.

I am grateful to the many journalists who shared their time and expertise; in particular I want to thank Kevin Anderson, Nick Bilton, Denis Burgierman, Gabor Vajda, and Derek Willis. Special thanks to my great friend Kerry Lauerman, who sat for many interviews with me over the years and whose smart and candid stories of his work as an editor have helped shape this book.

I would also like to thank the many friends and colleagues who offered advice, encouragement, and criticism over the years: Chris Anderson (the one at Indiana University not at *Wired*), Michela Ardizzoni, Rod Benson, Lynn Schofield Clark, Waddick Doyle, Nabil Echchaibi, Corinna di Gennaro, Ted Glasser, Jayson

Harsin, Alfred Hermida, Mimi Ito, Risto Kunelius, Merlyna Lim, Howard Rheingold, Tony Shawcross, Matt Tegelberg, and Barbie Zelizer. Many thanks to Liz Fakazis, a great and careful reader, for passing her eyes over every word and sending vital late-stage feedback.

Thanks to my mom, Jay Duchene, for her encouragement and for taking care of the kids while I traveled and for inviting me repeatedly and always with a smile to hole up in San Francisco to write. Thanks to Sammy and Sofia: World Champion Distractors.

Most of all, thanks to John Tomasic. His insight into his own work as a journalist greatly influenced my own understanding of where the field is and where it is going. More than that, his patient encouragement and practical help – talking through ideas and editing and reediting drafts of the book literally over the course of years – went far beyond the call of duty. It's not really possible to thank him enough.

1

Introduction

The Rise of Networked Journalism

The Gulf War was the best-covered war in history.
Dick Cheney (Frontline 1996)

Preface

Networked is about a transformative era in the history of media, the twenty-year period from 1990 to 2010, when the web rose and newspapers declined. The book centers on the transition as it has occurred in journalism. In networked journalism, members of various publics make journalism material that intersects, mixes, and is distributed to a new heightened degree. To me, networked journalism is journalism that sees publics acting as creators, investigators, reactors, (re)makers, and (re)distributors of news and where all variety of media, amateurs and professional, corporate and independent products and interests intersect at a new level. What's more, the variety of forms and perspectives that make up news in this environment and the number of connections linking creators to one another have significant influence on the news and have expanded journalism as a category of information and genre of storytelling.

Others have described networked journalism simply as collaboration between professionals and amateurs (Beckett 2008; Jarvis 2006; Rosen 2009). Jeff Jarvis (2006), journalist and author of the high-profile blog BuzzMachine, writes that in networked journalism, "the public can get involved in a story before it is reported, contributing facts, questions, and suggestions. The journalists can rely on the public to help report the story." Jarvis describes a trend where professional journalists accept input from the public while maintaining their authority over the news product, but this shift in the relationship between professionals and the public is just one element of the current changes taking place. Networked journalism is about more than journalists using a digitally equipped public as a kind of new hyper-source. It is also about a shift in the balance of power between news providers and news consumers. Digital publishing tools and powerful mobile devices are matched by cultural developments such as increased skepticism toward traditional sources of journalistic authority (Jenkins 2006; Russell et al. 2008). Contemporary journalism products and practices give new relevance to long-standing questions at the heart of what used to be called the journalism profession: How is truth defined and by whom? Which forms and practices of journalism yield the most credible product? How do consumers measure value among, on the one hand, elite media institutions, with their gatekeepers, resources, and professional codes and training, and, on the other, the bloggers and wiki-ists and emailers, with their editorial independence, collaborative structures, and merit-based popularity?

These questions became central to the debate about the 2003 Iraq War and about news of the war as it circulated on the internet, over the airwaves, and in print. Working at the time as a Networked Publics Fellow at the University of Southern California Annenberg Center for Communication, where my colleagues were researching new digital realities in youth and music and activist media cultures, for example, I came to view the heavily mediated culture of the news information industry as transformative, especially as I began to compare coverage of the 1991 war and coverage of the 2003 war. I grew to believe the similarities of the two eras underline the differences: there were two presidents Bush, two Persian Gulf wars, and two media environments.

The Old and New News

Gulf War 1991: High-Modernist Journalism

Coverage of the first Gulf War was characterized by the qualities of mass media – by the predominance of commercial and
professional news product and a one-way communication model
catering to a national community. Coverage of the second Gulf
War was characterized by qualities of networked media – by an
influx of independent and amateur news products and conversational models of communication organized around communities
of interest.

The first Gulf War was not just a mass-media story, not even
just another trademark mass-media story like Watergate or the
O.J. Simpson chase and trial. It was more a culminating kind of
story, an exclamation point to a chapter in communication history.
The address delivered by President George H. Bush the night the
war began, January 16, 1991, attracted the largest audience in the
history of American television. Nielson estimated that 78.8 percent
of the people in homes with television sets were watching and that
record numbers of those viewers stayed tuned as the U.S. Air Force
began its attack on Iraqi infrastructure (Carter 1991). The narrative
strategy adopted by the broadcast stations was to simultaneously
stoke the drama and sanitize the action. News staffs branded the
event with dramatic music and titles based on Pentagon operation
names like "Iraqi Freedom" and "Desert Shield." Editors flipped
among segments featuring Pentagon analysts, snapping and spar-
kling artillery over Baghdad, and fighter-plane footage of U.S.
smart bombs delivering themselves through windows and doors of
Iraqi buildings – technological footage that looked like a cerebral
video-game, where each of the bombs snaked over the city toward
the ground and ended in a silent flash. The intensity of the story
was heightened by the fact that its subject was the first-ever "real-
time" war, a media product made possible by new technology that
enabled reporters to beam video over satellite feeds.

The practice of journalism as developed and promoted in the
hundred years before the war – including sourcing preferences

where authorities dominated, narrative structures that privileged the status quo, the rise of visual media culture, and the widespread adoption of broadcast technology – yielded consistent coverage of the war at the major news outlets, producing, in effect, a single narrative across media, a narrative that was, it turned out, easy to manipulate. The first Gulf War is often cited as an example of the revolutionary "CNN effect" in action, an instance where a popular twenty-four-hour international news channel significantly influenced public opinion and government policy (Belknap 2001; Livingston 1997). The idea is that by focusing continuous real-time media coverage on a particular conflict, international incident, or diplomatic initiative, the news media increase public awareness and political attention and accelerate the policymaking process. The press, in its role as the so-called "fourth estate" in representative political systems, however, has always had an influence on public opinion and policy. The CNN effect simply describes the intensification of already existing relations. The introduction of the twenty-four-hour news cycle did not mark a revolution in news media but rather a culmination, where practices were exaggerated and relations intensified, the lines separating journalists from the sources of their stories and the companies they worked for becoming increasingly blurred as a matter of perception if not of fact.

The Narrative

After the fact, journalists lamented that they lost control of the Gulf War story, that they had been docile and easily shepherded by their sources. Mostly they said they had failed to properly follow the long-established codes of the profession, which, if followed, would have yielded more complex and accurate coverage (Massig 2004). The story they missed in their post-war mea culpa reporting, however, was the "perfect storm" of long-gathering professional, technological, social, and political conditions that made the first Gulf War the ideal mass-media news story, not a low point, from that perspective, but a high point, less an aberration than an inevitability.

Then-Defense Secretary Dick Cheney saw the war from that perspective, describing it as "the best-covered war in history."

> We provided more information in near real-time than ever before in history in any conflict. The press was not happy with the way we did it because a lot of it we did direct to the American people. Our daily briefings for example that were covered live on television. They didn't get to cover the war they wanted to cover but in fact the nature of modern combat, the fact you fight at dark at very high speeds across desert terrain, that means the old romantic notions of a reporter going out sort of traveling with the troops are a thing of the past and you have to, in fact, make arrangements for the press to cover that kind of an operation. It has to be done in conjunction with military and . . . I was interested in seeing that they got a chance to do their job but not at the risk of accomplishing the mission or at the risk of casualties to American troops. (Frontline 1996)

By "best-covered war," Cheney meant it was the most tightly controlled and spectacularly delivered war coverage ever produced. The relatively few outlets that delivered versions of the war alternative to the dominant narrative did not benefit from the institutional backing and channels of distribution that helped saturate the world with Cheney's "best-covered war." That narrative of events came almost entirely out of briefings organized by the military and attended by reporters from major news outlets the world over. In Iraq, as opposed to Vietnam, for example, very few reporters were allowed to visit the frontlines or to conduct interviews with soldiers, and those visits and interviews were conducted in the presence of officers and subject to both prior approval by the military and later security editing. Indeed, these "information management" tactics came as part of a public relations strategy designed to avoid a repeat of what the military viewed as the public relations disaster of the Vietnam War (Hatchen & Scotton 2006; Kellner 1992).

By almost all measures, the Pentagon's updated public relations approach had the intended effect on journalists as much as it did on the larger public. Opinion polls showed Americans overwhelmingly supported the war. According to a Pew survey (2003b),

77 percent felt the U.S. had made the right decision in attacking Iraq. One *LA Times Mirror* poll (1991) found that 50 percent of respondents considered themselves "obsessed" with war news and that nearly 80 percent felt the military was "telling as much as it could." Perhaps because the duration of the invasion was so brief (January 17, 1991 to February 28, 1991), support for the war and trust in the military remained consistently high. Americans also became part of the war news at the pro-war rallies that were covered nightly on television. Anti-war protests, however, received comparatively scant coverage, in terms of column inches and broadcast time. The protests didn't fit the narrative. They were made to seem aberrational or anti-American through context by editors who ran protest coverage alongside reports of anti-American demonstrations in the Middle East (Kellner 1992). On one side, viewers were presented with flag-waving choruses of pro-USA chants; on the other, flag stompings and burnings in effigy (Bishop 2006).

It was only much later that journalists, citizen groups, and official investigators succeeded in publicizing the extent and success of the Pentagon's control of the war narrative. Pressed for information, the military admitted a year later that many of the war's star weapons systems had not performed as well as reported. The Stealth bomber experienced technical difficulties and the Navy's Cruise missiles struck not 90 percent of their targets, as the Pentagon claimed at the time, but only 50 percent (Hatchen & Scotton 2006: 142). It was not until January 6, 1992 that John MacArthur, the publisher of *Harper's* magazine, revealed in a *New York Times* op-ed some of the facts surrounding the compelling testimony of a 15-year-old Kuwaiti girl identified only as Nayirah, whose allegations that Iraqi soldiers killed infant children in Kuwait were used to trump up support for the war. She had not been witness to a terrifying hospital raid by Iraqi soldiers. In fact she was the daughter of a Kuwaiti diplomat and her influential emotional Capitol Hill testimony was a fraud: the facts of the alleged raid had been exaggerated beyond recognition; and the Capitol Hill hearing itself had been a mock-hearing orchestrated by a PR firm and chaired by two sitting U.S. Representatives in its pay. But it all looked real on television. The Congressional setting, the men in suits posing questions behind microphones, and the tear-soaked testimony riveted television audiences primed to respond to the visual cues. Cable news flashed the testimony around the world as if it were taking place before a genuine committee hearing. Then-President Bush quoted Nayirah at every opportunity. Six times in one month he referred to "312 premature babies at Kuwait City's maternity hospital who died after Iraqi soldiers stole their incubators and left the infants on the floor," none of which was true (Ireland 1991) but all of which had been a very real news story.

High Journalism Brought Low

This perfect storm countered the goals of the mass-media news profession that emerged in the early 1800s in the United States, where newspapers were freed from reliance on political parties and touted as a potentially post-partisan educational medium that could bolster democracy. The advent of the penny press in 1833 signaled a new breed of newspaper based on a commercial model that sought mass readership (Schudson 1978; Schudson & Karl 1986). Benjamin Day, publisher of the first penny press paper, the *New York Sun*, expanded circulation of the paper by appealing to working-class readers with sensationalistic stories that dealt with the concerns of the masses. His writers reported on crime, local politics, natural disasters, labor struggles, and the cost of living, much of which had not been considered newsworthy previously. Advertisers were willing to pay for space and the *Sun* dropped its price from five cents to one cent, making it affordable to those outside the elite classes. The economic viability of sensationalism helped move newspapers away from reliance on political parties for financial support. The penny press industry brought in more advertisers and employees and intensified competition for news and for audiences.

But parallel to the rise of commercial news and mass circulation came the rise of professionalism (Schudson 1978; Schudson & Karl 1986). Research suggests the ideal of news objectivity came with the invention of the telegraph in the early 1840s and the subsequent birth in 1848 of the first American wire service, the Associated Press (AP). AP and other wire services attempted to produce reporting objective enough to be accepted by the politically varied papers that they served. Striving for objectivity did not, however, become the norm or practice in journalism until after World War I. Wartime propaganda and public relations campaigns convinced journalists that facts could not be trusted; that what they reported too often had been created for them to report by interested parties. Staged media events and the proliferation of government-sponsored information had shaped reporting and the opinions of reporters. In response, news writers formed an allegiance to rules and procedures alleged to result in objective reporting (Schudson 1978; Schudson & Karl 1986). According to journalism historian Michael Schudson, objectivity meant that "a person's statements about the world can be trusted if they are submitted to established rules deemed legitimate by a professional community" (1978: 7). The growing professional faith of journalists generated social cohesion and occupational pride, on the one hand, and internal social control, on the other. Journalists and editors, in effect, policed one another through promotion and lack of promotion, for example. By the 1920s, this pattern produced a self-conscious professionalism and a dominant ethic based on objectivity (Schudson 1978: 82).

Journalism scholar Daniel Hallin has famously referred to the subsequent era of American journalism – from the end of World War II until roughly the 1980s – as high modernism, and demonstrates that rather than being the natural or ultimate state of journalism, it was just a brief period based on very specific historical political, economic, and cultural conditions. Despite a rise in commercialism, journalists during this era were relatively free of commercial pressure, allowing for professional autonomy and dedication to social responsibility. In addition, unlike today, the period was characterized by a high level of ideological consensus in the United States centered on bipartisan agreement around Cold War foreign policy and the light corporatism and welfare state that emerged from the New Deal. This is in part why the objectivity norm developed more strongly in the United States than in continental Europe. This consensus, however, has long since been fragmented by the Vietnam War, conflict over race, gender, and sexuality, and hyper free-market economic policy, among other factors (Hallin 1992, 2000; Hallin & Mancini 2004).

In the 1960s and 1970s journalism and journalists reflected the increasingly polarized political landscape, responding and contributing to it by shifting to a more assertive stance, making their own role as political actors more apparent (Schudson 2003). Likewise, the shift from family to corporate ownership of newspapers, the deregulation of broadcasting, and the intensification of competition in broadcasting and between traditional and emergent forms of news media heightened the pressure on journalists to produce content that would attract more news consumers (Schudson 2003). Since the 1980s journalists have lost even more autonomy within news organizations increasingly dominated by market demands. Deregulation and the multiplication of channels have contributed to the strong reemergence of partisan media.

Hallin describes how professionalism receded, in part, because of a shift to "neoliberalism," determinist global market liberalism, and the activism this shift inspired. "For the Liberalism of the mid-twentieth century, professionalism acted as a balance to the logic of the market," he writes.

> Neoliberalism in contrast tends to be cynical about any claim about values that cannot be reduced to market choices. Neoliberalists deride the idea that journalists serve a higher purpose than that of the market as elitist language that clearly borrows from the very different critique of professionalism advanced by a variety of social movements, which aimed to shift power from elites to citizens. (Hallin 2006)

Indeed, the charge of elitism is used by those who would like to see the news media environment both more and less dominated by the market. Although Hallin precisely traces the conditions that spurred the end of this era, he also sees no reason to lament its passing: "It makes little sense to be nostalgic for the high modernist period of American journalism, which had many problems of its own, and which in any case belongs to a historical era that cannot be recreated" (2006: 2).

By now, the biases produced by the culture of objectivity are widely acknowledged. Analysts say that the rules of journalism developed during the high-modern era chiefly serve media corporations (Rashco 1975; Schiller 1981; Schudson 1978) and that the culture of objectivity demands fairness and balance but only within the limits of consensus or the "common sense" of a particular political system (Hartley 1982). Sociologist and political activist Todd Gitlin (2003), for example, argues that journalistic devotion to hard fact and editorial balance led to coverage of the Vietnam-era anti-war movement that emphasized confrontation rather than analysis of issues and shaped a portrayal of the movement as operating outside the boundaries of reasonable dissent. Hallin (2006) writes:

> [The] coincidence of forces in the decline of professionalism reminds us that the consequences of the decline are complex, and in some ways can be seen as representing greater democratization and greater responsiveness toward the concerns and perspectives of various parts of society, and in some ways the opposite, an increasing subjection of the institutions of communication to the interest that dominate economic life.

While the professional norms of mass-media journalism attempted to use objectivity to separate facts from values or opinions, journalism scholar Ted Glasser (1984) writes that these mechanisms for creating and maintaining truth create a predictable series of biases. First, he says, the norms of objectivity favor the status quo because they encourage reporters to rely on bureaucratically credible sources. He argues that White House sources, lawmakers, staffers, CEOs, and corporate researchers, for example, are all insiders by definition: their perspectives are limited to what works within the system, which they're not looking to change. Second, the professional norms discourage independent thinking because they dictate that journalists are mere spectators, compelling them to attempt to leave their own inevitable opinions and insights out of their stories. Third, norms of objectivity are biased against the idea of responsibility: the objectivity which journalists claim exists in their stories absolves them of accountability for the content. The mass-media news, with its strengths and weaknesses, delivered the Iraq War to national and international audiences as a tightly packaged and spectacularly performed event that left little room for interpretation and dissenting opinion.

Iraq War 2003: Post-Modernist Journalism

Administration and Pentagon efforts to control news of the Iraq War, which began in March 2003, were every bit as intense as those undertaken during the Gulf War. The George W. Bush administration, where Cheney was vice president, prized secrecy and information control (Boler 2008; Massig 2004) and spent billions of dollars on national and international public relations campaigns aimed at squelching opposition to U.S. forces in the Middle East and anti-Americanism generally (Hatchen & Scotton 2006). This time, in response to lawsuits journalists filed in the wake of the Gulf War, the Pentagon would "embed" members of the media with military units during operations. The military operation this time was called "Shock and Awe" and, like "Desert Storm" and "Desert Shield," it became a network news product brand name.

Amy Goodman, host of the syndicated daily radio and television news show *Democracy Now*, reported the way the government seemed to be building consensus for the war. The Gulf War of the 1990s had been pitched as a battle against dictatorial aggression and a move to protect Kuwaiti sovereignty. This time Goodman and others saw a "concerted effort to convince the American people that they should be afraid, that they were threatened, that there was an imminent threat" (Boler 2008: 200). White House Chief of Staff Andrew Card established an administration marketing team called the White House Iraq Group to sell the war by pushing the idea that Iraq posed a nuclear threat to the United States.

The campaign succeeded. Nearly all major national polling

organizations reported public support for military action in the 70 percent range during the first few weeks of the war. Perceptions of how well the war was going also were consistent across polling organizations (Pew 2003b). A Pew survey conducted during the first five days of the Iraq War found that 72 percent of Americans believed the decision to take military action against Iraq was correct, while 22 percent thought it was the wrong decision. The survey also found that public attention to news coverage of the war was on par with interest in the first Gulf War. About 79 percent rated Iraq War coverage as good or excellent, roughly the same number as during the Gulf War (Pew 2003a).

Seven months into the Iraq War, however, Gallup found that the percentage of Americans who viewed the invasion as a mistake had jumped substantially, from 25 percent in March 2003 to 40 percent in October 2003. Four years into the Iraq War, a February 2007 survey by the Pew Research Center for the People and the Press reported that public opinion about the war and about media performance in covering the war had plummeted. Most Americans now reported having little or no confidence in the information they were receiving – from either the military or the media. Fewer than half (46 percent) said they had a great deal or fair amount of confidence that the U.S. military was giving the public an accurate picture of the situation, and even fewer (38 percent) were confident in the media's war reporting (Dimock 2007).

The 1991 Gulf War lasted roughly one month. The Iraq War, however, dragged on for years after Baghdad fell and even after dictator Saddam Hussein fled and was captured, tried, and hanged. Information control broke down. Stories created by the White House Iraq Group began resurfacing in increasingly more thinly dissected versions. The dominant military narrative that the Iraq War would be a new kind of lightning war with limited casualties facilitated by U.S. technology fell apart as Iraqi society descended into sectarian violence and U.S. troops took on the role of public safety officials and occupiers. The resulting slogging chaos and absurdities were captured in quotidian detail, for example, by the student-made internet video series Hometown Baghdad, which was hosted by major U.S. online sites like Salon.com. The young video makers behind Hometown Baghdad were not embedded with American soldiers. They didn't go to U.S. military briefings. On the contrary, they knew the city and the country better than did any foreign journalist. Their video diaries went through virtually no editorial layers. They didn't run their recorded life-experiences past official or pro-war sources to balance them out with counter-interpretation. Hometown Baghdad matched with corroborating blogs coming from Iraq, like RiverBend, which called into question dominant news narratives at every turn. Soon the alleged links between Saddam Hussein and al-Qaeda were being called into question on the nightly news and in newspapers. The search for Saddam Hussein's alleged weapons of mass destruction turned up nothing. The heroic rescue of U.S. Private Jessica Lynch was revealed as farce.[1] News and images of U.S. military torture and Iraqi and U.S.-led coalition casualties began first trickling and then streaming out into the international mediasphere from alternative sources such as blogs and email and cell phones. What's more, some of the key producers of this alternative news product included members of the U.S. military: that is, Iraq War soldiers, who were more fully "embedded" with the Pentagon's operations than were any of the journalists on the ground but who were also much less heavily monitored, even though they owned the kind of frontline communications equipment reporters from any previous war zone could only have dreamed of possessing.

In the leadup to the war, activists and journalists online monitored mainstream media coverage. They critiqued what they viewed as tepid reporting of anti-war protests. In a study of the newscasts aired at ABC, NBC, CBS, and PBS during the two weeks leading up to the Iraq invasion, the watchdog group Fairness and Accuracy in Reporting found that of 393 interviews conducted, only three were with anti-war leaders (Boler 2008: 201). In that same period, however, millions of people in cities throughout the world were demonstrating against the war, part of the largest anti-war movement in history. Editors at major newspapers, including the *Washington Post* and the *New York Times*, responded to a critical email campaign by apologizing for not covering the protests and the anti-war movement more actively and for not featuring the protests more prominently in the weeks leading up to the start of the war.

One of the major media scandals of the Iraq War centered on the way the *New York Times* was manipulated into reporting the administration's line on the threat posed by Saddam Hussein's alleged weapons of mass destruction. In an extraordinary editor's note, the *New York Times* acknowledged errors in its reporting of the story:

> We have found . . . instances of coverage that was not as rigorous as it should have been. . . . In some cases, the information that was controversial then, and seems questionable now, was insufficiently qualified or allowed to stand unchallenged. Looking back, we wish we had been more aggressive in re-examining the claims as new evidence emerged – or failed to emerge. . . . We consider the story of Iraq's weapons, and of the pattern of misinformation, to be unfinished business. And we fully intend to continue aggressive reporting aimed at setting the record straight. (*New York Times* 2004a)

Many of the flawed stories were written by Judith Miller, a Pulitzer Prize-winning reporter who had covered the Middle East for years. Miller was later jailed for refusing to reveal the name of the anonymous source she relied upon for her Iraq weapons stories, Irving Lewis Libby. Critics accused Miller of crossing an ethical line by establishing close relationships with a small coterie of key Bush administration staffers, including Libby, and not seeking to verify the information they were feeding her. Miller went to jail, they said, to protect the identity not of a whistle-blower, for example, but of the operatives who had used her to publish their case for the war. The story she wrote based on the information she was getting wasn't true. Miller wasn't protecting a source. She was protecting herself against evidence that she had been played by the administration (Massig 2004).

Nevertheless, *New York Times* editor John Geddes in a fall 2005 speech to the Associated Press Managing Editors Conference described events surrounding Miller's reporting and defended the newspaper. He said it was journalism, not Miller, that the *New York Times* was protecting when it decided to back her decision not to reveal her source. Geddes's speech was impressive for the commitment it displayed to the ideals of the profession. Geddes defended the norms and codes guiding the profession by apologizing for not following them, which was his explanation for the bad coverage. The mistakes wouldn't have happened, he said, in effect, if we had only followed the rules.

The rules, however, had changed. The start of the Iraq War corresponded to the rise of the internet as a medium for professional journalism and analysis as well as for rapidly expanding user-generated content. By 2003, a vibrant field of readily accessible public communication had formed, for example, by academics, bloggers, citizen-sponsored journalists, and what journalism scholar Orville Schell (2004) called "second-tier news outlets." The new material augmented and often clashed with material produced by the mainstream media. Indeed, the second Bush administration soon seemed to be conducting wars in two theaters that it had not fully researched and did not understand: post-Saddam Hussein Iraq and the web-enhanced mediasphere.

In 1991, the year of the Gulf War, the World Wide Web had literally just been invented by Tim Berners-Lee. By the start of the Iraq War in 2003, according to a Pew Internet and American Life Project report released that year (Pew 2003a), 77 percent of Americans had used the web to find information about the war, to learn and share differing opinions about the conflict, and to send and receive emails where they pondered events, expressed their views, and offered prayers. Two November 2004 surveys by Pew determined that 8 million American adults said they had created blogs; blog readership jumped 58 percent in 2004 to 27 percent of internet users; 5 percent of internet users said they used RSS aggregators or XML readers to find news and other information delivered from blogs and websites; and 12 percent of internet users had posted comments or other material on blogs (Rainie 2005).

The story of Abu Ghraib, of the conditions maintained and the abuses carried out by U.S. personnel at the prison just west of Baghdad, is one of the emblematic networked news stories of the war. Personal digital media technology produced the evidence at the heart of the story and online news outlets were key in distributing that evidence as news. A 2004 report authored by U.S. Major General Antonio M. Taguba found sadistic, blatant, and wanton criminal abuse of Iraqis by American soldiers at Abu Ghraib. Considerable evidence supported allegations, Taguba wrote, including detailed witness statements and the discovery of graphic photographs and video taken by American soldiers. Taguba didn't include digital photos and video with his report but they became the primary source material for the news media once the story broke.

CBS news magazine *60 Minutes II* was the first to air the story in April 2004, using as one of its main sources a video diary created and emailed home by Army Reserve Staff Sergeant Chip Frederick, one of the perpetrators of the abuse. A few days later, the *New Yorker* published a story by Seymour Hersh (2004) on the prison and included photographs taken by U.S. military prison guards. The article was followed in the next two weeks by two more articles by Hersh on the same subject: "Chain of Command" and "The Gray Zone." The horrible, bizarre, transmittable, reproducible digital images of Abu Ghraib and the victims and the perpetrators of abuse there rocketed across the web. The *New York Times* (2004b), the *Boston Globe* (2004), and other outlets called for Secretary of Defense Donald Rumsfeld's resignation. The cover of the *Economist* (2004), which supported President Bush in the 2000 election, carried one of the digital snapshots with the headline "Resign, Rumsfeld."

Two years later, as the war and heated debate about the war dragged on, Salon.com obtained and published files and other electronic documents from a U.S. Army internal investigation report on the scandal that had been leaked to the press. The report included a review of

> all the computer media submitted to [the Army] office, including 1,325 images of suspected detainee abuse, 93 video files of suspected detainee abuse, 660 images of adult pornography, 546 images of suspected dead Iraqi detainees, 29 images of soldiers in simulated sexual acts, 20 images of a soldier with a Swastika drawn between his eyes, 37 images of military working dogs being used in abuse of detainees and 125 images of questionable acts.

According to Jeanne Carstensen, Salon.com's former managing editor, the internet was the perfect medium for the story:

> The Abu Ghraib package was a journalistic opportunity that comes along very rarely, and it was a perfect marriage of an extremely important journalistic story that had to be told, and the right medium to tell it in. It was perfect because creating galleries of those photos on the web was the best way that you could ever hope to present such an archive and we were able to build it in such a way that now exists as the definitive record of the Abu Ghraib scandal. (Unpublished interview 2007)

Salon.com had unlimited digital space to publish and archive the story and its supporting documents. These now live on the web as accessible and as clear as the day they were posted. Salon.com was free of the constraints that had reined in most of the traditional news organizations reporting the story, many of which published a minimum number of Abu Ghraib images, which they felt were too disturbing and controversial.

The story of prisoner abuse at Abu Ghraib is one among many instances where the loss of control of the story on the part of the Bush administration and the Pentagon echoed the loss of control of the story on the part of newspaper and television news editors and reporters and publishers. Members of the public on a whole new scale enjoyed direct access to the raw material of the news and the means to analyze, package, publish, and distribute it, and they did. That action changed the news and journalism in profound ways: stories filed by embedded reporters were trumped by soldiers' personal emails and photos; Western-trained journalists were criticized for lacking crucial knowledge of the cultures on which they were reporting; Western audiences surfed to Arab outlets to get news and to view footage absent from Western reports; independent reporters raised their own funding through online donations; satirical remixes of political speeches were created and circulated; independent websites posted images that mainstream outlets passed over; independent documentary filmmakers armed with low-cost digital tools shot, edited, advertised, and distributed their work online; and mainstream media were scrutinized and disinformation was exposed often within hours or days.

Networked: Technology as Culture; Journalism as Culture

The most obvious changes in the news media landscape over the twelve years between the Gulf War and the start of the Iraq War were the widespread adoption of the World Wide Web,[2] the proliferation of low-cost digital tools, and the ubiquity of digital networks. This, however, is not a book about technology. It is a book about how news is being transformed by the ways people are using technologies to find, create, organize, present, and circulate news and how conceptions of journalism and of the work of journalism and its purposes are expanding. Raymond Williams' (1973) concept of dominant, residual, and emergent products of distinct social and cultural structures reminds us that historically unique environments lead people to develop certain kinds technologies and to use them in historically specific ways. New technologies are adapted, tweaked, or hacked to meet prevailing needs (Brown & Duguid 2002; Hine 2000; Ito 2008).

Journalism is also a social construct. The best way to understand the field of journalism is to look at what news and news work means within the culture of journalism rather than attempting to study it from the outside as product or institution. Journalism historian James Carey famously calls for a departure from the "transmission" view of journalism to a "ritual" view, which understands communication as "a symbolic process whereby reality is produced, maintained, repaired and transformed." Drawing on the work of anthropologist Clifford Geertz (1973), he suggests studying communication as culture in order "to understand the meanings that others have placed on experience, to build up the vertical record of what has been said at other times, in other places, and in other ways" (Carey 1988: 62). Along these same lines, journalism scholar Barbie Zelizer (1992) argues that journalism should be considered not only a profession but also an interpretive community, where members are united by a shared discourse and by collective interpretation of key public events. In her analysis of coverage of John F. Kennedy's assassination, she demonstrates the process by which journalists interpreted events in a way that argued for their own (the journalists') legitimacy as storytellers. Journalism scholars Ted Glasser and James Ettema (1998) approach investigative journalism as a form of social and moral inquiry and use interviews with journalists to explore the tensions and contradictions that characterize professional mainstream American journalism. Sociologist Pierre Bourdieu (2005), in his analysis of the "journalistic field," argued that the journalistic product is primarily shaped by the ways members of the field negotiate among themselves. He contended that to understand journalism, one cannot look to readers' needs and expectations. Instead, he wrote, "the essential part of what is presented in [the newspapers] *L' Express* and *Le Nouvel Observateur* is determined by the relationship between *L' Express* and *Le Nouvel Observateur*" (2005: 45).

Most journalism scholars, however, have focused their attention exclusively on the culture and products of mainstream professional outlets, which is only a small and shrinking dimension of contemporary journalism. Zelizer writes, "Consider the repertoire of candidates that would not currently merit membership under the narrowed definition of journalism: A Current Affair, MTV's Week in Rock, internet listservs, Jon Stewart, nakednews.com, reporters for the Weather Channel, and rap music are a few that come to mind" (2004: 6). Media scholar Peter Dahlgren (1992) calls this the "metonymic character" of journalism scholarship, or the tendency to define journalism based on the study of only a small portion of news products and producers. Although scholars are widening their perspective as alternative news forms and news producers proliferate, an artificial division continues to separate the study of so-called "mainstream" and so-called "alternative" journalism and is manifest in the way scholars still mostly treat anything but traditional news practices as only tangentially related to news discourse (Russell 2007).

Studies that do consider alternative journalism, such as the research by the Goldsmith Leverhulme Media Research Center published in *New Media, Old News* (Fenton 2010), often measure it according to the elitist democratic model. This model is commonly associated with Walter Lippmann, an influential critic of journalism and celebrated journalist, a founding editor of *The New Republic*, and two-time Pulitzer winner for his syndicated column "Today and Tomorrow." Lippman saw the central role of the press as acting on behalf of the public as "watchdogs" of the powerful elite (Benson 2010). Journalism scholar Rodney Benson points out that, according to this model, new media exacerbate the crisis in journalism and thus in democracy, mainly because economic and institutional shake-ups have been met with a decline in "watchdog" or accountability journalism, especially at professional news outlets. That view, he argues, overlooks both the many new forms of accountability journalism being created, and the diverse functions of journalism beyond its watchdog role. Benson identifies three broad schools of thought in democratic theory – elitist, deliberative, and pluralistic – and argues that how we understand and evaluate journalism in the networked era depends on which of these democratic models are emphasized and valued.[3] He suggests that if we look beyond Lippmann's elite model of democracy, we can see more clearly the ways new media might support rather than corrode democracy. The deliberative model, for instance, sees journalists as facilitators, working to promote dialogue among members of the public through communication in which they are encouraged to participate. The aim here is to support reflection and robust understandings of news-related policies and issues in order to improve the quality of public life (Benson 2010; Christians et al. 2009). And the pluralist model sees journalists creating energetic engagement with diverse forms and perspectives to encourage *understanding across lines of difference* that empowers publics (Benson 2010; Bohman 2000). As examples throughout this book will illustrate, projects within and outside mainstream media outlets strive to make news a conversation among members of the public and journalists and to facilitate more dynamic engagement between and among diverse publics. Benson's astute analysis reminds us that our ideas about what forms and functions constitute journalism impede our ability to understand and effectively create the journalism of the future. If we judge journalism only by its role as a watchdog, for example, we overlook other equally important functions flourishing in the emergent environment, including journalism that facilitates deliberation and that enhances pluralism. By focusing on emergent cultural forms and practices related to journalism, the aim of this book is to expand the terms of debate around news, news publics, and the function of journalism as a democratic tool.

This Book

Networked identifies three aspects of the rise of networked journalism, which offer new or newly prominent possibilities for democratic engagement: amateur and non-market production; the role of niche and special-interest groups in opening up and "networking" the news environment; and the ascendance of the aesthetics of parody, remix, and appropriation.[4] These characteristics of the new news environment also serve as the organizing structure of the book. The book presents and critiques examples of these aspects of the networked environment and analyzes the way they influence news product, practices, and roles.

Between 2004 and 2010 I conducted interviews with more than sixty news media producers working in six different countries. I also interviewed journalism educators and followed conversations taking place online, in academic journals and at conferences. This study of and engagement with the culture and practice of journalists is combined with analysis of news content related to the case studies presented in the book. For the case studies where I examined various networked journalism products, I conducted qualitative analysis of content and commentary.

While many of the case studies, projects, and journalists informing the book are international in scope, its focus is primarily on U.S. developments, influenced by the U.S. blend of journalism history and cultural practices, industry organization, and concerns surrounding infrastructure and intellectual property issues. U.S. journalism is marked by advanced software development, for example, and limited but increasingly mobile phone penetration and mobile internet access (Varnelis 2008). I have found that the journalism culture in the United States seems relatively stubborn in clinging to traditional journalism models and practices. While researching this book, I have been made constantly aware of the fact that journalism is evolving along different trajectories depending on national, political, cultural, and economic contexts. This book in no way claims to cover the transition outside of the U.S. I have deliberately focused on the specifics of U.S. journalism, a variety that is broadly influential and significantly influenced by a more expansive emergent networked society and culture.

Networked employs an expanded definition of journalism and of journalists, one that reaches beyond the products and producers of traditional journalism that are typically the focus of academic work and public debate. Journalism here refers to the wealth of news-related information, opinion, and cultural expression, in various styles and from various producers, which together shape the meaning of news event and issues. Journalism has extended far beyond stories created for television broadcast outlets or for publication in traditional commercial newspapers and magazines. Journalism can be a conversation that takes place in the blogosphere; an interactive media-rich interface on a mainstream or alternative news site that provides context to a breaking story; the work of any number of fact-check sites; a tweeted camera-phone photo of a breaking news event; a comment or comment thread on a news site; a videogame created to convey a particular news narrative, and so on. In such an environment journalists are no longer strictly the people who gather information and create news stories from that information for a living.

The U.S. Senate in 2009 debated who should be able to call upon federal shield laws drafted to protect journalists from having to reveal confidential sources. The initial wording of the law focused on the craft of journalism over the business of journalism. The law identified a journalist as a person who:

(i) with the primary intent to investigate events and procure material in order to disseminate to the public news or information concern-

22

ing local, national, or international events or other matters of public interest, regularly gathers, prepares, collects, photographs, records, writes, edits, reports or publishes on such matters

(ii) has such intent at the inception of the process of gathering the news or information sought.

The revised definition broadened the scope to include people who work with a wide variety of media. These new journalists:

> Obtain the news or information sought in order to disseminate it by means of print (including, but not limited to, newspapers, books, wire services, news agencies, or magazines), broadcasting (including, but not limited to, dissemination through networks, cable, satellite carriers, broadcast stations, or a channel or programming service for any such media), mechanical, photographic, electronic, or other means. (Seward 2009)

Yet before the new shield law was adopted, the definition was further revised to apply to only those who "work as a salaried employee of, or independent contractor for, an entity." The final version excluded amateurs of any sort, including student reporters, bloggers with a day job, so-called "citizen journalists," and part-time and unsalaried news writers and broadcasters. This tendency to define journalism by its business model and by the technology through which it is distributed is not unique to lawmakers. In fact it is, as mentioned above, a major shortcoming of much of the journalism scholarship of the past decade, which has pitted old and new forms against one another, failing to recognize the ways new and old media and professional and amateur authors work in the same environment, influencing each other in form and content to shape the meaning of news events and issues (Seward 2009).

Cultural Narrative and News Transformations

Professional journalism norms have long been challenged by alternative or radical media products and practices created in opposition to the content and structure of mainstream news media products and practices (Atton & Hamilton 2008; Couldry 2000;

Downing 2000; Gitlin 2003). New media technologies and products from the printing press to satellite television have been touted for their revolutionary capacities. What's new in the networked era is the extent to which alternative forms are proliferating and overlapping with mainstream forms within the media landscape, which is partly the case because networked publics are developing connections with one another and expanding the sphere of legitimate debate (Hallin 1986). In the mass-media era, traditional news media largely defined the sphere of legitimate debate because the public was connected to the media but not to one another. Today it is much cheaper and easier for user-participants to find each other and exchange opinions and information. In doing so they often realize that the official news-generated sphere of debate doesn't reflect their own (Rosen 2009).

Chapter 2 is about a new public. Just as the telegraph transformed views of time and space and changed the way journalism was practiced, pushing it toward styles and forms that were appealing to geographically dispersed audiences, the proliferation of low-cost digital communication tools and networks has transformed the role of journalists and of the public. No longer merely news audiences or consumers, networked news publics are engaged – with each other, with news producers, and with news sources – in new ways. News publics are now practically aware that the mass-media of the past, which had come to seem natural, is not the only possible form.

The notion that there is a new more central role for news publics in the newsmaking process is the basis for one of the central cultural narratives surrounding the changing journalism landscape: the empowered publics narrative. Scholars like Henry Jenkins and Yochai Benkler, whose work has significantly shaped understanding of the news media environment both within and outside the academy, celebrate the rise of networked publics and their wide influence on media industries. Benkler (2006) theorizes that we are at the beginning of a shift away from commercial media and centrally organized knowledge production toward "non-market" and distributed production. He suggests that the network, with its "variation and diversity of knowledge, time, availability, insight, and experience as well as vast communications and information resources," has taken over the watchdog function of the press, ~ievahlv a peer-to-peer activity. Similarly, Jenkins

ties of spoiler groups for the reality television show *Survivor*. By gathering information from all over the world and communicating over the internet, networked fan groups collectively produce knowledge that far exceeds what local fan groups could muster. The information environment created though networked engagement extends beyond entertainment into news. He writes that "by pooling information and tapping grassroots expertise, by debating evidence and scrutinizing all available information, and perhaps most powerfully, by challenging one another's assumptions, the blogging community is spoiling the American government" (Jenkins 2006: 332)

Chapter 2 argues that changes in conceptions of journalism correspond to changing views of publics and demonstrates the ways both are shaped to varying degrees depending on the specific case by enduring notions of professional authority, new technologies, and market demands. While publics are now networked, and compelling examples exist of non-market production and of new forms of information gathering and engagement, these phenomena are not always reflected in how the public is being integrated into journalism products and practices. By examining the roots of what today has developed into broad-based participatory journalism, we can see the way various news organizations and projects are attempting to bring the audience into the production process and signaling various and shifting conceptions of the public. Drawing from interviews with journalists and editors involved in projects that experiment with amateur news production and/or audience participation at the BBC, the Huffington Post, France's Bondy Blog, among others, the chapter explores ways in which notions of the public and its relationship to news are changing. The chapter also demonstrates how networked publics are still very much shaped by the various conceptions of publics held at professional news outlets, which are by and large still reluctant to embrace the full participatory potential of the new environment.

Chapters 3 and 4 address the narrative of decline, a less hopeful yet equally powerful narrative that argues emergent technologies are eroding the quality of news and, thus, the quality of public culture. It is widely acknowledged that the economic decline of the news industry has reduced the ability of the press to produce accountability journalism, or journalism in which reporters investigate government and corporate wrongdoing (Fenton 2010; McChesney & Nichols 2009, 2010; Schudson & Downie, 2009). Media scholar Robert McChesney and journalist John Nichols argue that this is the single most significant development in journalism. In their book *The Death and Life of American Journalism* (2010), they declare democracy in crisis because of the state of the news industry. They blame corporations for creating frivolous and poor-quality news, the internet for forcing them to do so, and the government for not contributing significant financial support to deliver quality journalism. While they commend online journalism that generates quality original reporting like ProPublica and Talking Points Memo, they argue "these fixes are mere triage strategies" (McChesney & Nichols 2009). The cure, they believe, is government subsidies that will support a return to the journalism that has receded in recent years. For Cass Sunstein, legal scholar and current Administrator of the U.S. Office of Information and Regulatory Affairs, the problem is not exclusively lack of accountability journalism but what he describes as an increase in the personalization of news, which allows people to sequester themselves among likeminded people and avoid contrasting points of view or topics outside the realm of their interest. He argues that people should be exposed to material that they would not have chosen in advance because "unplanned, unanticipated encounters are central to democracy itself. . . . They are important partly to ensure against fragmentations and extremism, which are predictable outcomes of any situation in which like-minded people speak only with themselves" (Sunstein 2001: 9). Without this, he argues, we have become polarized – a political culture where people tolerate only those who share their own views.

Chapter 3 challenges this narrative of decline by examining how early attempts at personalizing the news have evolved. After

gence of so called   Web 2.0

an increasingly sophisticated intras
the chapter looks at changes in habits c
networked publics, and the ways these chc   - in
the coverage of the December 2009 United N   summit on
Climate Change, ultimately arguing that there has been a shift
from personalization to socialization of news, and with it new
potential for accountability journalism and for public engagement.

Chapter 4 further challenges the narrative of decline by suggesting that there are new or newly central forms of civic expression
that go unacknowledged by those who insist that the new news
environment is inferior to the old one. This chapter examines
the history of détournement as a political tool and argues that its
contemporary manifestations – remix and parody – have become
an increasingly significant part of the networked news landscape.
By examining popular contemporary news parody – including *The
Colbert Report*, *The Daily Show*, and The Yes Men – this chapter
argues that, contrary to the assertions of those who claim these
new genres signal cynicism and a breakdown of civic engagement,
these alternative discourses are both a product of and antidote to
the particular challenges faced by contemporary global culture
and are creating new forms of engagement that are acting partly at
least to revive civic culture.

Chapters 3 and 4 do not so much refute the demise narrative,
but rather suggest that there is more to the story. There is nothing
untrue about the arguments of those who worry about journalism
– accountability journalism generated by traditional news outlets
has declined in both quality and quantity; we are no longer collectively exposed to the same news; and contemporary political
polarization seems intense. These are important elements of the
shift in journalism to acknowledge and document, and to a great
extent my work builds on this scholarship. My quarrel with the
demise narrative and the scholarship that feeds it is primarily its
narrow focus and its amnesia over the shortcomings of the old
model that have been outlined in this chapter. My own point of
view has more in common with those who celebrate the potential

of the new environment as a basis for a revived public culture. We are not ever going to return to the professional and centralized news of last century, nor should governments subsidize any retreat to the past. On the other hand power structures that exist offline will not magically level off because of new tools and networks, and this book aims to explicate rather than gloss over tension between emergent and traditional journalistic practices, products, and institutions.

The final chapter suggests ways we can create and maintain the conditions necessary for a networked news landscape to flourish and meet the needs of the public, arguing that the future of journalism depends on our collective ability to create and accept new organizations, technologies, policies, practices, and ways of understanding our role in the new media environment.

Notes

1 Jessica Lynch publicly countered the story in the mainstream media that she was a war hero, telling Diane Sawyer: "[The Pentagon] used me to symbolize all this stuff. It's wrong. I don't know why they filmed [my rescue] or why they say these things." (http://www.cnn.com/2003/US/11/07/lynch.interview/). In 2007 she testified before the United States House Committee on Oversight and Government Reform that the Pentagon erroneously portrayed her as a "Rambo from West Virginia," when, in fact, she never fired a shot after her truck was ambushed (http://www.usnews.com/articles/news/iraq/2008/03/18/jessica-lynch-recalls-her-captivity-in-iraq.html).

2 The World Wide Web was invented 1989 by Tim Berners-Lee but it did not become a major tool of journalism until the mid- and late nineties, when newspapers began experimenting with putting their content online and when personal computers became cheaper and thus more widely used.

3 Several recent works have treated in-depth the various roles and functions of journalism, for example Clifford Christians et al. (2009) identify four press roles as monitorial, facilitative, radical, and collaborative. Michael Schudson (2008) writes of the six functions as being information, investigation, analysis, social empathy, public forum, and mobilization. While these characterizations differ from one another and from Benson's three theories of democracy and their corresponding roles of journalists, all have in common an acknowledgement of the press being more than a watchdog, emphasizing its various roles as a facilitator of discourse and of dialogue among various groups.

4 These developments are drawn from the essay "Networked Public Culture" (Russell et al. 2008).

28

Atton, C . & Hamilton, J.F. (2008) *Alternative Journalism*. New York: Sage.

Beckett, C. (2008) "Networked Journalism." *Guardian*, May 3. http://www.guardian.co.uk/commentisfree/2008/may/03/networkedjournalism

Belknap, M.H. (2001) "The CNN Effect: Strategic Enabler or Operational Risk?" U.S. Army War College Strategy Research Project. http://www.iwar.org.uk/psyops/resources/cnn-effect/Belknap_M_H_01.pdf

Benkler, Y. (2006) *The Wealth of Networks: How Social Production Transforms Markets and Freedom*. New Haven: Yale University Press.

Benson, R. (2010) "Futures of News." In: N. Fenton (ed.), *New Media, Old News*. London: Sage.

Bishop, C. (2006) "The Social Turn: Collaboration and Its Discontents." ArtForum, February. http://www.artforum.com/inprint/id=10274

Bohman, J. (2000) *Public Deliberation: Pluralism, Complexity, and Democracy*. Cambridge, MA: MIT Press.

Boler, M. (2008) "Introduction." In: M. Boler (ed.), *Digital Media and Democracy: Tactics in Hard Times*. Cambridge, MA: MIT Press.

Boston Globe (2004) "Rumsfeld Must Go." *Boston Globe*, May 7. http://www.boston.com/news/globe/editorial_opinion/editorials/articles/2004/05/07/rumsfeld_must_go/

Bourdieu, P. (2005) "The Political Field, the Social Science Field and the Journalistic Field" (R. Nice, Trans.). In: R. Benson & E. Neveu (eds), *Bourdieu and the Journalistic Field*. Cambridge: Polity Press.

Brown, J.S. & Duguid, P. (2002) *The Social Life of Information*. Boston: Harvard Business School Press.

Carey, J. (1988) *Communication as Culture*. Boston: Unwin Hyman

Carter, B. (1991) "War in The Gulf: The Networks; Giant TV Audience for Bush's Speech." *New York Times*, January 18. http://www.nytimes.com/1991/01/18/us/war-in-the-gulf-the-networks-giant-tv-audience-for-bush-s-speech.html?pagewanted=1

Christians, C.G., Glasser, T., McQuail, D., Nordenstreng, K., & White, R.A. (2009) *Normative Theories of the Press*. Champaign: University of Illinois Press.

Couldry, N. (2000) *The Place of Media Power: Pilgrims and Witnesses of the Media Age*. New York: Routledge.

Dahlgren, P. (1992) "Introduction." In: P. Dahlgren & C. Sparks (eds), *Journalism and Popular Culture*. London: Sage.

Dimock, M. (2007) "Who Do You Trust for War News." Pew Research Center for the People & the Press. April 5. http://pewresearch.org/pubs/445/who-do-you-trust-for-war-news

Downing, J. (2000) *Radical Media*. New York: Sage.

Economist (2004) "Resign, Rumsfeld." *Economist*, May 6. http://www.economist.com/node/2647493

Fenton, N. (ed.) (2010) *New Media, Old News*. London. Sage.

Frontline (1996) "Oral Histories: Interview with Richard Cheney." The Gulf War: An Indepth examination of the 1990–1991 Persian Gulf Crisis. http://www.pbs.org/wgbh/pages/frontline/gulf/oral/cheney/1.html

Geertz, C. (1973) *Interpretation of Cultures*. New York: Basic Books.

Gitlin, T (2003) *The Whole World is Watching*. Berkeley: University of California Press.

Glasser, T. (1984) "Objectivity Precludes Responsibility." *The Quill*, February, 13–16.

Glasser, T. & Ettema, J. (1998) *Custodians of Conscience*. New York: Columbia University Press.

Hallin, D. (1986) *The Uncensored War: The Media and Vietnam*. Los Angeles: University of California Press.

Hallin, D. (1992) "The Passing of the 'High Modernism' of American Journalism." *Journal of Communication* 42:3, 14–25.

Hallin, D. (2000) "Commercialism and Professionalism in the American News Media." In: J. Curran & M. Gurevitch (eds), *Mass Media and Society*. London: Arnold.

Hallin, D. (2006) "The Passing of the 'High Modernism' of American Journalism Revisited." Political Communication Report. International Communication Association & American Political Science Association, Vol. 16, No. 1, Winter.

Hallin, D. & Mancini, P. (2004) *Comparing Media Systems: Three Models of Media and Politics*. New York: Cambridge University Press.

Hartley, J. (1982) *Understanding the News*. London: Methuen.

Hatchen, W. & Scotton, J. (2006) *The World News Prism: Global Information in a Satellite Age*. New York: Wiley-Blackwell.

Hersh, S. (2004) "Torture at Abu Ghraib American Soldiers Brutalized Iraqis: How Far Up Does the Responsibility Go?" *New Yorker*, May 10. http://www.newyorker.com/archive/2004/05/10/040510fa_fact

Hine, C. (2000) *Virtual Ethnography*. London: Sage.

Ireland, D. (1991) *Village Voice*, March 26.

Ito, M. (2008) "Introduction." In: K. Varnelis (ed.), *Networked Publics*. Cambridge, MA: MIT Press.

Jarvis, J. (2006) "Networked Journalism." BuzzMachine, July 5. http://www.buzzmachine.com/2006/07/05/networked-journalism/

Jenkins, H. (2006) *Convergence Culture*. Cambridge, MA: MIT Press.

Kellner, D (1992) *The Persian Gulf TV War*. Boulder, CO: Westview Press.

Livingston, S. (1997) "Clarifying the CNN Effect: An Examination of Media Effects According to Type of Military Intervention." Harvard University Kennedy School of Government Joan Shorenstein Center for Press and Politics.

McChesney, R. & Nichols, J. (2009) "The Life and Death of the Great American Newspaper." *The Nation*, March 18.

Introduction

McChesney, R. & Nichols, J. (2010) *The Life and Death of Great American Journalism.* New York: Nation Books.

Massig, M. (2004) *Now They Tell Us.* New York: New York Review of Books.

New York Times (2004a) "From the Editors." *New York Times*, May 26. http://www.nytimes.com/2004/05/26/international/middleeast/26FTE_NOTE.html?scp=1&sq=Editors%20Note%205/26/2004&st=cse

New York Times (2004b) "The New Iraq Crisis; Donald Rumsfeld Should Go." *New York Times*, May 7. http://www.nytimes.com/2004/05/07/opinion/the-new-iraq-crisis-donald-rumsfeld-should-go.html

Pew (2003a) "The Internet and the Iraq War." Pew Research Center for the People & the Press, April 1. http://www.pewinternet.org/Reports/2003/The-Internet-and-the-Iraq-war.aspx?r=1

Pew (2003b) "Polls in Close Agreement on Public Views of War." Pew Research Center for the People & the Press, April 2. http://people-press.org/commentary/display.php3?AnalysisID=64

Rainie, L. (2005) "The State of Blogging." Pew Internet and Amercian Life Project. http://www.pewinternet.org/Reports/2005/The-State-of-Blogging.aspx

Rashco, B. (1975) *Newsmaking.* Chicago: University of Chicago Press.

Rosen, J. (2009) "Audience Atomization Overcome: Why the Internet Weakens the Authority of the Press." PressThink, January 12. http://journalism.nyu.edu/pubzone/weblogs/pressthink/2009/01/12/atomization_p.html

Russell, A. (2007) "Digital Communication Networks and the Journalistic Field: The 2005 French Riots." *Critical Studies in Media Communication* 24:4, 285–302.

Russell, A., Ito, M., Richmond T., & Tuters, M. (2008). "Networked Public Culture." In: K. Varnelis (ed.), *Networked Publics.* Cambridge, MA: MIT Press.

Schell, O. (2004) "Preface." In: M. Massig, *Now They Tell Us.* New York: New York Review of Books.

Schiller, D. (1981). *Objectivity and the News.* Philidephia: University of Pennsylvania Press.

Schudson, M. (1978) *Discovering the News.* New York: Basic Books.

Schudson, M. (2003) *The Sociology of News.* New York: W.W. Norton & Company.

Schudson, M. (2008) *Why Democracies Need an Unlovable Press.* Cambridge: Polity Press.

Schudson, M. & Downie, Jr., L. (2009) "The Reconstruction of American Journalism." *Columbia University Review*, October 19. http://www.cjr.org/reconstruction/the_reconstruction_of_american.php

Schudson, M. & Karl, M. (eds) (1986) *Reading the News.* New York: Pantheon Books.

Seward, Z. (2009) "Shield Law: House and Senate Differ on Who's a Journalist," September 17. http://www.niemanlab.org/2009/09/shield-law-house-and-senate-differ-on-whos-a-journalist/

Sunstein, C. (2002) *Republic.com*. Princeton N.J.: Princeton University Press.

Varnelis, K. (ed.) (2009). *Networked Publics*. Cambridge, MA: MIT Press.

Williams, R. (1973) "Base and Superstructure in Marxist Cultural Theory." *New Left Review*, November–December. http://www.newleftreview.org/?issue=81

Zelizer, B. (1993) *Covering the Body: The Kennedy Assassination, the Media, and the Shaping of Collective Memory*. Chicago: University of Chicago Press.

Zelizer, B. (2004) *Taking Journalism Seriously: News and the Academy*. New York: Sage.

2

Participatory Journalism

The Wealth of Networks

> Only the Pulitzer committee can preserve the journalism priesthood now.
>
> Gawker (Tate 2010)

Journalist versus Journalist

It stands there on Pennsylvania Avenue on the Mall in the nation's capital, a steel and glass modernist masterpiece that through architectural magic conjures an idealized high-tech version of a street-corner newspaper box, or maybe a boxy television from the height of the network-television era. It took six years and roughly $450 million to create this new, larger, high-tech version of the Newseum, a national shrine to the history of American news media. Joe Burris of the *Baltimore Sun* voiced a popular opinion of the museum when it opened in 2008: "It's one of the best things that has happened to the profession in years. . . . It's an innovative way to foster fascination and respect for truth-gathering and truth-telling" (Newseum Website 2008). Funded by major news corporations including Knight, Bloomberg, the New York Times Company, Comcast, Hearst, ABC, NBC, and Time Warner, the Newseum seems at once to celebrate industry stewardship of professional news practices and products and to acknowledge that professional mass-media news is already receding, joining the ranks of the dinosaur bones located in the Smithsonian across the

33

green. The Newseum may have been "one of the best things to happen to the profession in years" because the evolutionary, and many would argue great, things happening to the field of journalism over the same six years the Newseum was being built were clearly not so good for the journalism industry as we know it.

Indeed, the museum opened just as the networked news environment was coming of age and signaling the end of an era. That year's presidential candidates, including Barack Obama, built on the prototype strategies of earlier grassroots or "netroots" campaigns like the one launched by Vermont governor Howard Dean in 2004. Dean impressed campaign analysts with the way his staff used the internet to gain supporters and raise money. In the 2008 contest, Obama and other candidates used digital media such as YouTube and Facebook to raise unprecedented sums of money, but also to effectively circumvent professional journalists and communicate directly with the public. What's more, non-professionals with laptops and digital cameras broke some of the major primary campaign stories at alternative news sites, shifting news and campaign narratives and demonstrating the power of distributed amateur reporting on a mass scale. The news public had changed but the perception of the public that had helped define professional journalism through the majority of the twentieth century had not, a fact not fully recognized or appreciated by the Newseum or by the outlets and industry it was built to celebrate.

In addressing the internet, the Newseum's Bloomberg Internet, TV and Radio Gallery declares: "No longer are the newspapers, radio, and TV the main gatekeepers of the news. . . . Today the role is shared by everyday people using new digital tools to act as eyewitnesses and help capture stories." This friction-free version of the reality that was shaping the news industry as audiences gained access to digital tools and networks is pervasive among many professional journalists and news organizations and it wrongly feeds the notion that they can embrace the new news environment, and are doing so, without fundamentally changing their own practices.

Cultural, economic, and technological changes in the news industry and in cultural industries more generally suggest otherwise. By 2008, an intense blogosphere had come to constantly turn over the latest news, analyzing it and fact-checking it and opining about it by the minute, across all subject matters, from foreign affairs to celebrity fashion. Voters had come to routinely post video from campaign events. Crowds sent instant messages covering unfolding events in real time. Activists remixed political speeches. It was all journalism and some of it was even recognized as news. In 2009, a cell phone video taken anonymously of a dying Iranian election protester named Neda, who was murdered by authorities on the street, rocketed first around the mobile web and then into the larger mediasphere before in 2010 the person who filmed it captured the prestigious George Polk Award for journalism – the first-ever anonymous winner (Stelter 2010). "Only the Pulitzer committee can preserve the journalism priesthood now," wrote the gossip writers at the popular website Gawker the day of the controversial award announcement (Tate 2010).

Indeed, traditional news industry professionals continue to treat this "citizen" or "civilian" activity alternatively as a sideshow, distraction, menace, and mystery. It is only recently that publishers and editors began to act on the idea that audience participation can be a resource, although they continue to defend their resistance to the full potential of participatory media. They maintain, for instance, that citizen sources present serious fact-checking questions and that effective investigation, particularly on an international scale, requires resources and organizational and political clout that lay-people bloggers don't enjoy. They also say that only corporate media have the financial resources to stand up to governments and corporations to uphold the public interest (Netanel 2002). Some of that is certainly true, but this way of thinking misses the point. The genie is out of the bottle; the public is off the couch. Collaboration is the resource to embrace now, one more valuable than institutional backing in almost all cases (Gillmor 2004; Rosen 2006b).

Media scholar Pablo Boczkowski argues that new media are revolutionizing the news industry not through technological change but, rather, by merging the structures and practices of existing media with newly available technical capabilities. "The news moves from being mostly journalist-centered, communicated as a monologue, and primarily local, to being increasingly audience-centered" as audiences become more involved in the production of content (Boczkowski 2005: 138). Jessica Clark and Pat Aufderheide (2009), directors of the American University's Center for Social Media, which tracks and analyzes emergent forms of public media, suggest that this shift in the journalism landscape has great potential in new media to revive public life:

> When Thomas Jefferson said that he would rather have newspapers without government than government without newspapers, he was talking about the need for a free people to talk to each other about what matters. When American philosopher John Dewey argued that conversation was the lifeblood of a democracy, he meant that people talking to each other about the things that really affect their lives is what keeps power accountable. When German philosopher Jürgen Habermas celebrated the "public sphere" created by the French merchant class in the eighteenth century, he was noting that when non-aristocrats started to talk to each other about what should happen, they found enough common cause to overturn an order.

Despite claims that this new model is beneficial to both publics and business – that consumers of news can more directly shape the news product, making it more relevant to the public and thus more viable as a profit enterprise (Gillmor 2004) – the fact is that there remains a fundamental tension between professional and commercial news models and emerging news products and practices. At the root of the tensions is the professional view of the public. Journalism is being redefined inside and outside mainstream news institutions, by professional journalists as well as by new actors who are experimenting with news platforms and delivery systems, content, practices, and norms. Definitions of journalism are changing but so too are definitions of what Jay Rosen (2006a) has called "the people formerly known as the news audience." New perceptions of the public inform new journalism projects and platforms and are shaping the qualities of networked journalism that will emerge as the public more fully enters the newsmaking process.

This chapter demonstrates that while publics are indeed now networked, and compelling examples exist of non-market production and of new forms of information gathering and engagement, these phenomena are not always reflected in how the public is being integrated into journalism products and practices. By examining the roots of persistent perceptions of the public as passive, as well as the more recent history of what today has developed into broad-based participatory journalism, we can better understand the factors influencing the ways various news organizations and projects are attempting to bring the audience in to the production process and how this signals various and shifting conceptions of the public. Drawing from interviews with journalists and editors involved in projects that experiment with amateur news production and/or audience participation at the BBC, the Huffington Post, and France's Bondy Blog, among others, the chapter samples the various ways notions of the public and its relationship to news are changing. The cases also demonstrate how networked publics are still very much shaped by the various conceptions of publics held at professional news outlets, which remain reluctant to embrace the full participatory potential of the new environment. This reluctance is in part due to the enduring commitment within many journalism outlets to the elitist view of democracy that sees the primary role of the journalist as monitoring the power elite on behalf of the public. Several of the cases here suggest, however, that despite this limited view of the public, its involvement offers possibilities for creating a more dynamic and democratic journalism environment.

Altered Perceptions of News Publics

Mass-Media Era: One-to-Many

Perceptions of the public that developed around mass-media news reflect the technologies that fostered so-called "one-to-many communication," where the direction of information mostly flows one way. As the printing press, radio, and then television became the primary media through which journalism was distributed, the nature of the public's relationship to news shifted from active to passive. Nineteenth-century printers decided what was news and delivered it to readers. As printing technology improved, the relationship between the news product, the producers, and the readers or viewers stayed the same. As I have proposed in Chapter 1, that paradigm culminated in the international news story of the 1991 Gulf War, where millions of people sat watching the CNN live broadcast version of the story. CNN's Gulf War story was the ultimate experience of one(CNN)-to-many(all of us) news.

Mass-media news eclipsed forms of hyperlocal news that had previously been the norm – news that came in the form of pamphleteering, for example, letter writing, local newsletters, and salon-style or public square-style conversation. The shift in technologies brought about a shift from a conversational mode of communication to one-way broadcast-style communication. The one-to-many or one-way model fostered journalism shaped by the norms and procedures of objectivity. As guiding principles, the norms of objectivity present themselves as an "enduring commitment to the supremacy of the observable and retrievable facts" (Glasser 1984: 13). Many see objectivity as a method by which journalists arrive at the "truth," to be delivered to a public that is seen as passive and overwhelmed by everyday life and is mostly incompetent in matters of discerning the value of information. Walter Lippmann thought very little of the public's ability and desire to analyze complex issues. He likened the average American to a "deaf spectator" who "doesn't know what is happening, why it's happening and what ought to happen" (Lippmann 1922: 13), and argued for an elite class of professionals who would sort out issues of public concern for a passive news audience. American philosopher and educator John Dewey wrote in a review of Lippmann's book *Public Opinion* published in the *New Republic*: "The manner of presentation is so objective and projective, that one finishes the book almost without realizing that it is perhaps the most effective indictment of democracy as currently conceived ever penned" (Dewey 1922: 286). Lippmann's vision is not only an indictment of democratic ideals, it also keenly reflects mass-media news norms and practices that were only just beginning to take shape when he made his observations. The norms and practices associated with this elite model of journalism largely construct the public as a group of passive consumers of news collected and delivered to them by professionals trained in the art or alchemy of objectivity.

The idea that the quest for objectivity should be abandoned in favor of acknowledgment that various journalists are narrative makers with subject knowledge, personal histories, and points of view is not new, but the idea has gained traction in conversations about journalism in the networked era. Writing in the 1960s, Hannah Arendt argued that storytelling "reveals meaning without committing the error of defining it, that it brings about consent and reconciliation with things as they are" (1968: 105). Stories, as opposed to official reports, encourage interpretation because what is presented does not claim to be truth but observation. What makes that idea particularly relevant in the networked era is not only that versions of news stories proliferate on the web but also the fact that the ability to observe life, as opposed to the ability to report news, has never been the exclusive domain of professionals. In the late 1980s James Carey wrote in defense of maligned mass-media news consumers, "members of the public will begin to reawaken when they are addressed as a conversational partner and are encouraged to join the talk rather than sit as spectators before a discussion conducted by journalists and experts" (1987: 14). Needless to say, members of the public have irretrievably joined the talk.

Just twenty years ago, we can now see, the talk was trapped in the mass-media paradigm. The 1980s were, in fact, a low point in the relationship between the press and the public in the United States (Fallows 1997). The convergence of companies created a mediasphere owned by only a handful of corporate conglomerates; public mistrust of the media and politicians ran at an all-time high, owing in part to a perceived elitism among members of the press; negative campaigning and horse-race coverage dominated coverage of the 1988 presidential election, which also saw record low voter turnout; and newspaper readership began a long and steady decline. Journalism was failing both as business and as public service. In the early 1990s, just before the development and widespread adoption of the internet, a small group of U.S. journalists and scholars sought to reform the relationship between the public and the press by treating readers and community members as participants in the newsmaking process. The movement came to be known as public journalism or civic journalism; its main proponents included Jay Rosen, New York University journalism professor, W. Davis "Buzz" Merritt, Jr., a former editor of *The Wichita Eagle*, and David Mathews, president of the Kettering Foundation. Public journalism stressed journalism's responsibility toward public life and argued that rather than being neutral and detached observers, journalists should act as advocates of public life by using the newspaper as a forum for community issues, by talking with people in the community and by covering issues that concern them (Glasser 1999).

That journalists should be advocates for anyone, however, raised alarms among more than a few traditionalists dedicated to the norms of objectivity and the neutrality they were meant to ensure. Writing in the *New Yorker*, David Remnick argued that "when journalists begin acting like waiters and taking orders from the public and pollsters, the results are not pretty" (1996: 56). Leonard Downie, executive editor of the *Washington Post*, wrote that "too much of what's called public journalism appears to be what our promotion department does" (Case 1994: 14). Despite criticism, however, public journalism was by no means a radical departure from traditional professional norms and practices in the field. Just as traditional journalism practices were formed on the idea that the public needed professionals who were uniquely qualified to present the truth, public journalism privileged professionally derived versions of reality. Although it advocated inviting everyday people into the conversation, it left journalists in charge of that conversation, seeing them as enlightened news directors who would decide which voices would be included and how reality would be presented. At the time, there was a burgeoning alternative and activist journalism movement that included news weeklies in cities across the country and progressive political magazines like *Mother Jones* and the *Utne Reader*. Most of these outlets, however, functioned outside the mainstream media – as advocates for the public interest rather than as voices of the public. Journalists were using the public as fuel for their various agendas rather than allowing the public to set the agenda and to participate in producing the news.

Networked Era: Many-to-Many

At roughly the same time that the public journalism movement was taking off, another movement emerged that in the end had much greater implications for the news media landscape. In 1990 the Association for Progressive Communication (APC) was founded with the goal of providing communication infrastructure, including internet-based applications, to groups and individuals working for social and environmental justice and sustainability. APC pioneered the use of digital networks as tools for advancing social movements and civil society and it was the first internet provider in many member countries. It changed the way progressive community organizations worked by setting up NGOs and individual activists with low-cost email, online discussion software, mailing lists, and the web. By 1995, APC oversaw more than 800 electronic "conferences" or online conversations on everything from AIDS to Zimbabwe. Participants publicized events, prepared joint proposals, and disseminated information and up-to-date news and perspectives. APC and its activist network forerunners significantly impacted international relations, as was the case when the Chinese government attacked student protesters in 1989. Chinese students used fax, telephone, and computer networks to transmit real-time and detailed accounts of the Chinese government massacre near Tiananmen Square, as well as to organize protests, raise money, and create support networks around the world. The impact of these communication networks was so powerful that the Chinese government began cutting telephone lines and monitoring computer conferences where much of this communication activity was taking place (Frederick 1992: 226).

In subverting government snoops and in some cases the traditional news media, these new international activist networks influenced the news environment by creating and circulating alternative versions of events and analyses of issues unhampered by the traditional forms and practices – including editorial and publisher gatekeeping – that define mainstream media. The networks had no editors to please and no media profits to maintain. They reported events raw and exploited emergent digital tools and networks to facilitate a more deliberative and pluralistic communication environment around these news-related topics.

One of the earliest and most dramatic examples of one such digital issue-based network is the international collection of emailers and listserv participants that formed around the Mexican Zapatista revolutionary movement of the 1990s. Beginning on New Year's Day 1994, the day the North American Free Trade Agreement took effect, the Zapatistas launched an armed struggle against what they saw as transnational free market capitalism run amok and destroying the agrarian economy and lifestyle in mountain state Chiapas and beyond. The Zapatista support network created and distributed alternative and mainstream media coverage of rebel clashes with the government (Castells 1997; Cleaver 1998a 1998b; Froehling 1997; Knudson 1998). Harry Cleaver, a University of Texas professor and participant-observer in the network, described these web-based forms of alliance-building as a new phenomenon and argued that the communication that emerged around the movement was spurred by a more active public. Zapatista network participants scrutinized information and countered disinformation in real time, writing their own critiques, updates, reports, and opinions. Like sociologist Manuel Castells (1997), Cleaver (1998a, 1998b) described the web as an answer to the dissident or outsider isolation that had been a product of media marginalization and that had minimized effectiveness of activist movements in the past. The Zapatista network accelerated communication and extended information outside traditional journalism institutions, taking a share of the power normally reserved to mainstream media.

The information-age activism of the Zapatistas looked like blogging before the dawn of the blogosphere. The most frequent posts in the listserv-based network contained mainstream news stories surrounded by rebuttals, item-by-item assessments, fact-checking corrections, contradictory reporting, and alternative readings, mostly produced and circulated by members of the support network rather than by journalists. Although journalists at major outlets at the time were often unaware of and able to ignore the network critiques of their work, Zapatista-network-style communication is exactly the sort of material integral to the news cycle today, its integration heightened by the prevalence of digital media and by the speed and efficiency of mobile communications and email and instant-messaging campaigns (Russell 2005).

The Zapatista movement initiated a trend toward alternative digital news networks (Castell 1997; Cleaver 1998b) that stemmed first from activist movements and later from groups not necessarily associated with specific causes or movements. In 1999, the Seattle Independent Media Center (IMC), a collective of independent media organizations and hundreds of journalists offering what they described as "grassroots non-corporate coverage," used the internet to support and coordinate protests against World Trade Organization meetings held there that year. The IMC site featured constantly updated multimedia reports on the protests and the protesters' clashes with police, reports uploaded mostly by amateur or what came to be known as "citizen journalists." Before the protest, IMC consulted with Harry Cleaver for tips on how to get people involved in creating and circulating information and joining a networked-based movement. IMC spurred Indymedia centers in cities throughout the world – the IMC public-as-journalist model became the prototype for varied experimental participatory news projects.

The emergence of the alternative news media in the last decade has challenged the controlling posture toward the public established by Lippmann. Journalists today can no longer ignore network communication – and largely because it has transformed the role of the news audience from a mostly passive to an active force. Web publishing tools, social networking sites, and powerful mobile devices have facilitated the move among growing percentages of the public toward active participation in the creation and dissemination of news. Non-professionals generate a sea of news product by the hour – for the benefit of news publics and journalism professionals. Indeed the era of the mythic "parasitic blogger" – that object of newsroom disdain caricatured as perpetually pajama-clad and feeding off the work of professionals – has suddenly receded. The information streams now clearly run both ways, as Maureen Dowd unexpectedly revealed when she was called out in May 2009 for cutting and pasting for her *New York Times* column the work of blogosphere icon Josh Marshall of the website Talking Points Memo (Tomasic 2009). Amateurs present challenges and opportunities for the news business. They are a two-way bridge to the heart of the public. They live everywhere and they're always on. Amateurs extend the reach of traditional journalists as de facto researchers and reporters, and they expand the mediasphere exponentially in the quantity and quality of information available.

New Approaches to Old Sources

Professional journalists now use social networking technologies like MySpace, Facebook, and Twitter, which have drawn millions of everyday users, to connect with the public, find story ideas, and contact sources. In his 2008 presidential election coverage for the London *Guardian*, Kevin Anderson, for example, created a distributed reporting network, using the popular networking tools Flickr, Delicious, and Twitter in addition to Facebook, to build contacts, connect and collaborate with fellow journalists, and conduct real-time reporting and aggregation. In a post describing how these tools aided in his reporting, he explained how he made contact with the public using multiple platforms:

> I posted my images to Flickr under a Creative Commons attribution-non-commercial use license,[1] which I felt was important because I was using Creative Commons licensed photos from Flickr to help illustrate my posts. I contacted fellow Flickr users to let them know I had used their pictures, something I try to do as a matter of courtesy and also as a lightweight way to promote our journalism. Sometimes those contacts developed into stories and contacts beyond the original posts. For example, I used this excellent photo of a foreclosed home in California

by Jeff Turner, who organizes property shows there. He followed me on Twitter and helped me find local contacts for my reporting on the housing crisis. (Unpublished interview with author 2008)

Anderson also used Twitter to connect and collaborate with journalists. He found out about increasing homelessness and tent cities in Seattle from blogging and tweeting journalist Monica Guzman of the *Seattle Post-Intelligencer*. "I doubt I would have learnt of any of that without her help. She pointed me to details on the *Seattle P-I* site, saving me valuable time" (Anderson 2009). Twitter also served as a real-time reporting tool and newsfeed for Anderson. On the night of the U.S. election, instead of going back to his hotel to finish his stories, he stayed in the street to follow the celebrating crowds. "I didn't have to wait until I got back to my hotel to report. I could report live from the streets, providing pictures (albeit grainy) and quoting the crowds as they chanted outside of the White House: 'Whose house? Whose house? Obama's house! Obama's house!'" (Anderson 2009).

As reporters begin to take up new networking tools and practices, newspapers are establishing related ethical guidelines. The *New York Times,* for example, focuses on maintaining an air of professionalism consistent with traditional definitions of appropriate practice: "If you have or are getting a Facebook page, leave blank the section that asks about your political views, in accordance with the Ethical Journalism admonition to do nothing that might cast doubt on your or *The Times*'s political impartiality in reporting the news" (Poynter 2009). *New York Times* editors explained the reasoning behind the guidelines to reporters by noting that "anything you post online can and might be publicly disseminated, and can be twisted to be used against you by those who wish you or *The Times* ill." The guidelines also offer advice on who to "friend" or connect with on Facebook. "A useful way to think about this is to imagine whether public disclosure of a 'friend' could somehow turn out to be an embarrassment that casts doubt on our impartiality" (Poynter 2009).

Projecting an image of impartiality in order to maintain the appearance of neutrality remained a priority. The *New York*

Times also addresses ethical questions that arise in the blurred private and public space journalists enter when using the new technologies for sourcing and information. "Approaching minors by e-mail or by telephone, or in person, to ask about their or their parents' private lives or friends is a particularly sensitive area. Depending on the circumstances, it may not be advisable" the paper tells reporters (Poynter 2009).

In the wake of the 2007 shooting spree at Virginia Tech, for example, students used Facebook to contact friends, exchange news and experiences, and mourn victims. An ABC reporter posted this: "Our thoughts are with everyone affected by the horrific tragedy at Virginia Tech. In our ongoing coverage, we want to speak with people that knew [gunman] Cho Seung-Hui. We have anchors and producers on campus that would love to meet with you" (Goodin 2007). And an NBC *Dateline* reporter wrote:

> We understand how difficult this is, and want to help share your story. "Dateline" NBC urgently looking for anyone who knew Seung Hui Cho. We have producers and camera crews nearby ready to talk to anyone who can supply information about him and his movements leading up to the tragedy. We are attempting to produce a thoughtful and informative report that might shed some light on the tragedy and possibly help prevent something like this from happening again. (Goodin 2007)

The way news media had turned to Facebook to find sources and storylines for their coverage of the shooting prompted resentment among some of the students, who felt reporters were trying to capitalize on their grief by eavesdropping on their personal conversations. Virginia Tech student journalist Courtney Thomas told the *Guardian* newspaper, "You have reporters that will create a Facebook identity just to get students' contact information or who will start an online memorial to get people posting for a story. It's just inappropriate" (Johnson & Clarke 2007).

Coverage of the Virginia Tech massacre was also heralded as a milestone for citizen media. It is a featured example in the Newseum's Bloomberg Internet, TV and Radio Gallery. A panel describing the coverage reads: "Mainstream media teamed with digital technology and citizen journalists to deliver the breaking news." Poynter Online likewise encouraged journalists to take note: "If you ever had a doubt about how important it is for your newsroom to be able to tap into user-generated content, the Virginia Tech story will change that" (Tompkins 2007). The failure of the Newseum exhibit to explore the question of whether the Virginia Tech coverage represented an exploitation of the public demonstrates a common assumption on the part of news organizations that the public is nothing more than a resource to augment professional reporting.

Networked Journalism Projects and Platforms

News organizations and projects, attempting to incorporate the formerly-known-as-audiences, construct new roles for the public based on perceptions of what the public is capable of and how participation fits into larger organizational economic and/or social goals. The following cases demonstrate perceptions of the public that are emerging as news organizations experiment with public involvement projects launched at the BBC, the Huffington Post, the French site Bondy Blog, and the social news sites NewsTrust and NewsCred.

Build It and They'll Come: The BBC's User-Generated Content Hub

The BBC is at once one of the most innovative news organizations and one of the most traditional: it has taken an aggressive approach to adopting new technology but remains paternalistic in its posture toward the public. It aims to increase public participation while preserving professional norms and practices. Members of the public are invited to be involved in the newsmaking process in order to add value to the product but implicit is the familiar vision of the public as passive and the truth as something that is discovered rather than created.

As the largest broadcaster and newsgathering system in the

world,[2] the BBC's adoption of new technologies and practices is a model for the news industry. A universal fee paid by all U.K. households with televisions funds BBC programming. There is, therefore, a direct fiscal relationship between the service provider and the consumer, but without any way for the consumer to assert preferences. Indeed, until very recently the organization created content without input from the public, while at the same time holding up public interest as its guiding principle. BBC editorial guidelines are unsurprising because they typify the view that dominated twentieth-century journalism: "Our specialist expertise will bring authority and analysis to the complex world in which we live. We will ask searching questions of those who hold public office and provide a comprehensive forum for public debate" (Horrock 2009). This guiding vision is strongly tied to the attitudes of the first director-general, John Reith, who, like Lippmann in the United States, had little faith in the ability of most members of the public to identify for themselves the information they would need to effectively engage in public life. "Few [readers] know what they want, and very few want what they need," wrote Reith (Congdon et al. 1992).

With the rise of private broadcasting stations, decreasing trust in journalists, and an increased desire and ability on the part of audiences to contribute to newsmaking processes, the BBC has faced what many have called a crisis of legitimation and accountability to the public (Born 2002).[3] As part of its effort to re-establish public trust and demonstrate the economic viability of its traditional model and practices, the BBC is adopting new digital communication tools and creating participatory projects that invite contributions from the publics they serve (Hermida 2009; Pete Clifton, unpublished interview with author 2008).

The BBC website BBCi was launched in 1997. By the time the newsroom was integrated in July 2008, the website was ranked by Alexa Traffic Rank as the twenty-seventh most popular English-language website, and forty-sixth most popular overall. The early version of the site did little more than make print and broadcast content available. The BBC was slow to add unique content to its website and to adopt platforms and policies that allowed the public to engage with news content and journalists. The BBC Action Network, which started in 2003 as iCan, was a grassroots online civic engagement initiative, which provided a space for establishing and organizing local groups. The Action Network was not designed to channel public voices into BBC news products but rather to give members of the public space to engage with one another. In the main section of the site, the campaign section, anyone can broach topics that concern the local community, from crime reports, for example, to updates on street and sanitation projects. Every campaign is organized and tagged both geographically and by issue (for example, "crime prevention" or "local policy"), so people browsing the website can find a campaign associated with their location or with an issue that concerns them.

Between 2003 and 2006, the BBC spent £1.3 million on the project and in 2008 it closed the Action Network because, according to BBC News Editor Peter Horrock (2008), "the level of involvement compared to the cost was inappropriate" and because the emergence of blogs and social networking platforms had made the project redundant:

> The whole web is now there for anyone with a special interest to pursue their cause easily. We have learnt from experiment and are now pointing users to alternative ways, inside and outside, of getting their voices heard. The general conversation on the web is freely available to all. The BBC does not have to host that either.

Alfred Hermida (2010), former editor for the BBC website, criticized the project for being based on a broadcast model. Instead of working with existing groups, he said, the BBC simply set up a big building and said, "You come to us and do what we think you should do." Hermida points out that web communities are difficult to create; they need to be nurtured, he said, and professional journalists are not trained in community organizing.

Things shifted in 2004 when a series of tsunami devastated the Indian Ocean coastline and people reached out to the BBC in mass numbers, sending emails, photos, videos, and audio files. Inspired editors set up a permanent User-Generated Content (UGC) Hub. Pete Clifton, BBC's head of editorial development for multimedia journalism, explains that user-generated content incorporated into BBC stories is heavily moderated to verify authenticity: "It's gone through all the filters that our journalism would have gone through. It's quite labor intensive. We have another arm of our newsgathering operation – it can ultimately add to the richness of what we do, but we shouldn't take it lightly" (Hermida 2008). The UGC Hub now has a team of fourteen journalists working to generate and manage content, using message boards and email forms to generate stories, case studies, and eyewitness accounts of events from all over the world. They also sort, verify, and share reader responses for use at the various BBC news departments. Eliciting audience input essentially functions as an extension of the reporting process. Matthew Eltringham, assistant editor of interactivity, for example, refers to the "Dodgy Petrol" story of 2007 as a groundbreaking example of BBC viewers and listeners shaping a story. In April of that year the BBC got a call from a local radio station saying people were complaining that their cars were running badly and that mechanics suspected spoiled petrol was the cause:

> We ran a story asking people to let us know if they had similar problems and things went absolutely bananas. We got thousands and thousands of people telling us that they had exactly the same problem. And it turned out that Tesco had got a dock load of petrol and initially they had done some tests and said "No, there's nothing wrong with our petrol." We were able to turn around and say "Actually there is something wrong with your petrol." All of these people cannot be wrong. . . . I'm sure this story would have come out at some point two weeks later as a slightly funny story in one of the papers. But it was our story. We took control of the story. (Eltringham, unpublished interview with author 2007)

As he describes it, the UGC Hub was able to leverage the public to help in the process of reporting and to raise the prominence of the story. Eltringham cites as another example of the public's influence on the news agenda the uproar over the Archbishop of Canterbury's comment that de facto inclusion of certain aspects of Sharia law in Britain seemed "unavoidable" (BBC 2008):

We ran a story and it was on the front page about half way down. Yeah it was there, but it wasn't really a story that really registered. So we asked for a little feedback and people just went absolutely ballistic. In three days we got about 35,000 comments. People desperately want to have their say about things like that. . . . Eventually after about four phone calls, and about ten thousand emails, BBC editors realized that perhaps they should lead on it, which is what they did. It was the lead in every single one of the papers the next day. (Eltringham, unpublished interview with author 2007)

Despite an eagerness on the part of BBC audiences to voice their opinion and engage in debate around news-related issues, the future role of the public at the BBC will likely focus on leveraging the audience to help report stories, according to Clifton: "Over the next two or three years, soon, we'll probably do less of the debating – like asking people to send in comments on issues – and more focus on getting added value that the audience can give to us. People value the BBC and they want to help us with our news-gathering" (unpublished interview with author 2007). Eltringham explains that the BBC is striving not to create community but to increase interaction between journalists and members of the public, which ultimately improves news quality by accelerating the process of reporting and expanding the spectrum of stories, subjects, and sources.

These views correspond to BBC's 2008 Statements of Programme Policy, which spelled out a plan to allow professional journalists to elicit, process, and publish contributions from the public in order to offer first-hand accounts and a wide range of views: "We aim to make it as simple as possible for audiences to make these contributions and create one seamless BBC News proposition across all platforms" (BBC 2008/9). The overall approach is about creating technical, editorial, and managerial processes that allow professional journalists to work more closely with the public.

Yet public material remains rigorously processed. The dodgy petrol and Archbishop of Canterbury stories demonstrate that BBC user-generated content can influence story selection and content, but the layered architecture ensures industry personnel remain at the center of news production and distribution. The BBC's "user-generated hub" is an elaborate gatekeeping operation. Audience voices are solicited at the same time as the sphere of legitimate discourse is kept tightly under the control of journalists and editors. Members of the public are seen merely as eyewitnesses with potential value. This of course challenges the notion that new tools and incentives to integrate the public into the news process are fundamentally changing the traditional dynamics between professional journalists and the public. The case of the Huffington Post offers an example in which the public has a very different but perhaps equally limited role.

The Huffington Post Gets Off the Bus

Off the Bus (OTB), a collaboration between Jay Rosen's Newassignment.net and the Huffington Post, aimed to bring citizen perspectives into coverage of the 2008 presidential campaigns. Jay Rosen launched NewAssignment in July 2006, aiming to spark innovation in "open platform" journalism, distributed reporting, and crowdsourcing, or web-enabled mass collaboration. Ariana Huffington and former America Online executive Kenneth Lerer founded the Huffington Post in May 2005. The now-mega traffic blog and aggregator site is often held up as one of few successful news enterprises at a time of industry crisis. According to Nielsen NetRatings, the Huffington Post attracted 8.9 million visitors in February 2009 and, according to Alexa.org, a popular web metrics site, it is the ninety-second most visited site on the web among Americans. In 2007, Rosen and Huffington launched OTB with a skeleton crew who would be experimenting in ways to rally Americans around the country into contributing material and in ways to present that material to the news-reading public. The success of the project – in garnering readers, breaking news, and influencing the larger media narratives of the campaigns – brought attention and legitimacy to the idea of citizen reporters. It also revealed new areas of tension between professional news practices and values, on one side, and emerging news products and methods, on the other.

OTB viewed members of the public as journalism outsiders – as interested observers barred from riding the real and metaphorical campaign buses and so able to offer valuable alternatives to traditional mainstream media campaign coverage and report information based on what they decided was news. OTB moved beyond the view of the public as journalism assistant by recognizing and exploiting unique layperson perspectives. Rosen believes that an emerging model that pairs amateurs with professionals in a hybrid journalism can leverage the unique perspective of citizens while maintaining a high-quality news product. By facilitating so-called "pro–am" partnerships, OTB attempted to create new-style journalists who could be inserted into the context of traditional journalism but could continue to challenge the norms of the profession. OTB "citizen journalists" acted as reporters, sometimes writing their own stories and sometimes contributing to distributed or "crowdsourced" reporting projects. At its height, OTB had more than 12,000 "citizens" generating content for the site and just four editorial staffers to manage, edit, fact-check, and post content (Huffington & Rosen 2008).

The national campaign was seen as a perfect story with which to experiment, the kind of story that moves across the country and that matters to voters everywhere but that can easily resolve into a few simple storylines developed and shared among journalists early in the race. Digital citizens who would be asked to contribute cash to the campaigns online could also be asked to contribute campaign coverage to OTB online. Rosen envisioned members of the public powering a journalism upgrade by pushing the boundaries of professional news culture. Project Director Amanda Michel, a former Howard Dean campaign staffer, described the OTB vision in the *Columbia Journalism Review* after the project wrapped: "Digital technology had broken the monopoly on the production of journalism, and we exploited that reality by organizing thousands of 'ordinary' (more often extraordinary) people to cover what was possibly the most important election of our lifetime" (2008: 42). OTB Managing Editor John Tomasic explained the implications of breaking the journalism monopoly:

We tapped into a whole new set of questions to frame our coverage, questions that sometimes had us scratching our heads: "Is this something?" We [professional journalists] are so used to following our own narratives, which have more to do with each other than with the public. At OTB we were handed new questions and we also gained new sources. Our reporters didn't have access to politicians and campaign officials so they had to find other people to call up and talk to in their lives and on the campaign trails – sources that ended up being more fruitful from our perspective than your standard spokespeople and operatives, partly of course because those kinds of sources were talking to [all the other news outlets]. (Unpublished interview with author 2008)

One of OTB's most prolific and high-profile reporters, Mayhill Fowler, describes the experience of finding her place among local and national media:

I came in with no preconceptions but over time I saw what a bad job the national media were doing. They were in such a bubble. There was no one there like me. I was with the local press and they turned out to be a huge resource for me. The national media would just fly in for the day: "Where are we?" We all knew the stump speeches by heart, so for [the national reporters] speech time was time to do other stuff – answer email, make calls, read blogs and other coverage. I mean, how can you do coverage like that? I would be out there talking to the crowds, to the local reporters, finding out what the major issues were in that state or town. (Unpublished interview with author 2008)

But OTB's citizen reporters created tensions as professional models were breeched at the high-traffic site. OTB, for example, was thrust into the national and international news spotlight when Fowler reported comments that Barack Obama made at a San Francisco fundraiser about "bitter" small-town Americans let down by politicians who "cling to guns or religion or antipathy to people who aren't like them." Fowler was at the fundraiser as a citizen not as a reporter. Obama's remarks stood out to her as emblematic of a larger Obama communication problem, an opinion she had developed by reporting on the campaign in states across the country and at a variety of events. Her essayistic story on the fundraiser, which attempted to express her feelings and put the comments in context, rocketed from the web onto television and into the newspapers. Overnight, Fowler became the face of a new-media revolution and her report brought up anxiety about changes in the news media landscape. The story posted on Friday, April 11, 2008, received more than 250,000 page views by the end of the day, and was picked up by all the major U.S. news outlets, including the *New York Times*, the *Los Angeles Times*, the *Washington Post*, CNN.com, the Associated Press, Fox News, Reuters, Politico, *Lou Dobbs Tonight*, *Hardball*, *Keith Olbermann's Countdown*, the Atlantic.com, DailyKos, and Talking Points Memo. It was the top story on Google News. Republican candidate John McCain and Obama Democratic primary rival Hillary Clinton quickly responded, trying to leverage the controversial remarks to benefit their campaigns. Obama released a video to respond to the controversy (Rosen 2008).

The Obama campaign was caught off guard by the changing news landscape and the new role of citizen reporter. The campaign, however, never contested Fowler's right to report what happened at the fundraiser or the accuracy of the quote. Obama supporters, on the other hand, rancorously accused Fowler of trying to bring down the campaign. She was in fact an Obama supporter and financial contributor. Fowler later thought she should have made that clear from the beginning:

> In June 2007, I knew Obama was going to be president. I knew it and that drove my coverage. I believe you should always hold anyone who runs for public office to the very highest standards. It's really the highest honor for them. And I really don't know why I never told readers until my very last post that I was sure he was going to win. The whole time I knew it. And all of my reporting was in that context, of my certainty. (Unpublished interview with author 2009)

Contemporary professional norms demand journalists avoid having or at the very least avoid revealing their political affiliations. In writing for the Huffington Post, Fowler was adopting, at least semi-consciously, the posture of professional journalism. In hindsight, she thought she made a mistake in doing so, in not being forthright about her support for Obama, which she believes would have underlined her efforts to be fair in her reporting. On the other hand Fowler's double identity as supporter and reporter to some constituted an egregious lack of transparency.

A few months later, in June 2008, Fowler hit gold again. This time in tiny Milbank, South Dakota, where she reported Bill Clinton's ranting response to a question she posed at the rope line at a Hillary Clinton rally. Fowler asked what the former president thought about what she called the "hatchet job" published about him that month in *Vanity Fair*. The controversy around Fowler's story on the exchange centered on debates over whether or not she had identified herself as a reporter. "I think we can safely say, he thought I was a member of the audience," she told Jay Rosen (Steinberg 2008). There was also debate about her wording of the question and whether by describing the *Vanity Fair* story as a "hatchet job," Fowler had falsely given Clinton the impression that she was a fan of his. As former Senior Writer Alex Koppelman argued in Salon.com's political blog War Room:

> I just can't see him saying what he did if he thought he was on the record with a reporter – indeed, he didn't say it to any other reporter. You can argue that in the age of the Internet, the ability of so-called "citizen journalists" to report these kinds of unguarded moments is a good thing, and that's an argument I tend to sympathize with, but the lines become really murky when that "citizen journalist" is someone like Fowler, working with an organization like the Huffington Post. (Jouvenal & Koppelman 2008)

In Koppelman's mind, Fowler had shown herself to be crafty and prolific and the Huffington Post, of course, was a major platform from which she was helping shape major news stories and campaign narratives. She was not the pajama-clad unbacked Blogspot-blogger who would come to mind when you think "Milbank citizen journalist," as perhaps Clinton was imagining. Responding to the Salon.com critiques, Rosen (2008) wrote:

> Newsroom people, hear me out. You don't have to leave the moral universe you grew up in. Just admit the possibility of another valid

one beyond yours. "Trust me because I mask my true feelings about the matter" is not an inherently better way to journalize or gain cred. "Trust me because I show you what my true feelings on the matter are . . ." can also work. And in certain settings – blogging, "citizen journalism," pro–am projects like Off The Bus – [that posture] is a more plausible, more workable and more believable means of bidding for the user's trust. (Also less expensive.)

In both cases Fowler introduced a new journalism to both the public and news media professionals, a journalism where being neutral or apolitical was not a requirement, and also where transparency was clouded. In the splash she made, grabbing off-kilter quotes from unguarded public figures and posting them to a heavy-traffic news site, for better or for worse, it was suddenly clear that the public could play a major role in the newsmaking process and was reworking norms and practices of journalism in the process. Fowler sparked controversy by acting at once as a supporter and a reporter, and in both cases the issues at stake for journalists and readers were transparency and neutrality. If Fowler were not an Obama supporter, she would not have been invited to the fundraiser, and if she had not described the *Vanity Fair* article as a "hatchet job," Clinton might not have sensed an invitation to do a hatchet job of his own. The responses to Fowler's stories clearly demonstrated the chaos caused by the shifting norms and roles of journalist/citizens, a chaos that the Huffington Post gladly capitalized on.

In the case of OTB, the public, while unwieldy and in need of professional guidance, was, according to its creators, politically activated by being asked to create journalism, and this citizen activism benefited journalism. Michel wrote that the editors of the project "discovered that politically involved people make great sources, especially en masse. . . . The timing for a new social contract between the press and the public could not be better. There will be no reason to mourn the loss of its audience if the press fully understands and exploits the new reality that its audience can now be its ally" (2009: 44).

Michel and Rosen believe that citizen journalism works under the "pro–am" journalism model, where professionals maintain control of the process and the product, creating new-style journalists who post product shaped in the context and style of traditional journalism but who also challenge the norms of the profession. It was Fowler's ability to leverage the freedom to break the rules that made her the star, but the coverage was still largely shaped by its relationship to the larger news landscape. Thus what was meant to be an effort to facilitate political deliberation and the inclusion of a plurality of voices and perspectives turned out to spur deliberation about the political reporting and resulted in coverage that closely adhered to the agenda of the traditional news media outlets. OTB wasn't trying to train away the amateur-ness of its contributors. On the contrary, the fact that the contributors were amateurs made them a valuable journalism resource. The case of France's Bondy Blog demonstrates how a similar model can play out very differently in a different context.

Bondy Blog Expands French Journalism with Banlieue Bloggers

Bondy Blog was the invention of Swiss magazine *L'Hebdo* during the 2005 riots and protests in France sparked by the death of teenagers Bouna Traore and Zyed Benna while being chased by police in the Paris suburb of Clichy-sous-Bois. While journalists from *Le Monde*, *Libération*, and other mainstream news outlets within and outside France struggled to gain access to cover the explosive banlieues, Bondy Blog set up an office there in an attempt to access views and perspectives of banlieu residents and to counter dominant coverage in the national and international press, which exclusively reflected the perspectives of the political and cultural elite in France. Mainstream coverage of the riots emphasized the perspectives of conservative politicians, namely the then Interior Cultural Minister Nicolas Sarkozy, who characterized the rioters as flagrantly unpatriotic *voyoux* or hooligans, whose outlaw behavior constituted a secession from France. Coverage was also full of racial and religious coding, which pushed potential emotional buttons of fear and hatred of immigrant and second-generation French populations in the recent historical context of debates about Islam in France, or the "headscarf issue"; and the present context of global Islam extremism, a recent history of terrorism, and right-wing alarms that the French banlieues were a breeding ground for terrorists (Felouzis et al. 2005).

L'Hebdo used its blog to post in-depth analyses by the reporters in Bondy. The public was encouraged to comment. *L'Hebdo* editors chose the best excerpts to publish in the print edition and later sent aspiring youth from Bondy to Lausanne for a week-long training workshop funded in part by French-language radio and television broadcast corporation Television Suisse Romande and Radio Suisse Romande. Announcing the program on its new "Bondy Blog," *L'Hebdo* acknowledged the irony of what it referred to as the "Bondy Blog Academy," a thinly veiled effort to diversify the news by exploiting Bondy youth for "bloggy" ethnic content – content prized for at least seeming to be raw, diverse, and unfiltered. The Bondy bloggers had no other journalism training than the extemporized *L'Hebdo* "academy," but they gained immediate access to major news audiences.

Bondy Blog staffers believe the 2005 rioters resorted to violence in part because they lacked a forum to express their view of events – a forum that would break the sort of news colonialism in place. The story of the banlieues, the French suburb slums populated largely by North African Muslims, has been reported for decades by white French professionals with little knowledge of the cultures upon which they are reporting. Bondy Blog was different in part because reporters there shared with rioters' anger and disillusionment with the neglectful political system (Echchaibi 2009). Paul Ackermann, one of the Swiss journalists who worked at the blog during its early phase, said Bondy Blog changed his understanding of events:

> I had the same view of French banlieues as anybody else from outside. I saw images of fire and it looked like war, too dangerous and violent. Once there, it was all different because we were learning to know people. The burning cars, buses, and buildings were the result of a malaise; not the beginning of a civil war. They were acts by youth revolted by the system, an epidemic reaction not legally acceptable, but these kids didn't know how to express their frustration otherwise. (Huynh 2009)

Although other high-profile citizen journalist projects like Indymedia, which hosts citizen media in cities throughout the world, focus on a broad range of topics over diverse geographies, Bondy Blog is hyperlocal, focused specifically on residents of the Paris banlieues, people who have been systematically excluded from public discourse. Bondy bloggers write about their own experiences in the banlieue. They also act as local reporters interviewing and blogging about Bondy residents and their perspectives; about local politicians and their proposed solutions to what ails the banlieue; and about the views and stories of their friends and neighbors who can give context to the banlieue, which after the riots became a major issue in the 2007 presidential elections. Media scholar Nabil Echchaibi writes:

> From this niche position, the blog selects, discusses, and comments on political, economic and social issues. Its ability to chronicle both the positive and negative sides of the banlieue as well as its role in the 2007 presidential elections, in which candidates made unusual campaign stops in the banlieues, have won the blog critical acclaim both in France and abroad. (2009: 11)

By including Bondy residents in the newsmaking process, Bondy Blog has opened an unprecedented space for otherwise unsolicited voices to participate in public discussions and feel a part of a mostly exclusive French white identity. Nordine Nabili, the blog's chief editor, says: "I would challenge anybody to find 10 percent of the topics Bondy Blog covers anywhere in the French media. The banlieue is simply a story of crime, delinquency, school problems, and unemployment. We go beyond this façade to talk about the root causes of these issues" (Echchaibi 2009: 21). Bondy Blog founder Serge Michel says that the mainstream media was initially very enthusiastic because they didn't recognize Bondy Blog was presenting a challenge and signaling a shift in the French news industry:

> They thought it was simply a project to help the banlieues and the youth who live there, and after the riots of November 2005, everybody was ready to help the banlieues. Later, they realized they were in

competition. The daily *Libération*, for instance, is opening local blogs and also [*Le Monde*'s site] Le Monde.fr, [where the] emphasis is on citizen journalism. And the relations between these two publications and Bondy Blog have become much more fresh. (Echchaibi 2009: 21)

In 2007 Bondy Blog entered into partnerships with Yahoo France and the popular free newspaper and news site "20 Minutes." Some of the posts published on Bondy Blog also now appear in both the print and online publications of 20 Minutes, extending even further the coverage of the banlieues. It has also started editions out of various other cities within and outside of France, including Marseille, Lyon, Lausanne, and Dakar. It has become a model of convergence between old and new forms of journalism. Bondy Blog editors notably argue for the credibility of the blog by emphasizing its ties to professionalism.

In a talk at the University of Colorado's journalism school in 2008, Editor-in-Chief Mohammed Hamid emphasized Bondy Blog's connection with professional journalists and offered assurances that the content is "serious" and that it doesn't recklessly cast off professional norms. Hamid's apologetic tone with regard to the involvement of non-professionals reveals an enduring view of the public as a threat to credibility, best kept away from the vital workings of the newsmaking process – even though in the case of Bondy Blog, the public creates the product. The public is seen as valuable in practice but a potential liability, partly in this case because Bondy Blog is still largely depending on the mainstream media to pick up and disseminate the voices of the banlieue. The value of the amateur Bondy contributors depends on the extent to which they can be transformed through training into journalists and their contributions can be transformed through editorial filters into a recognizable, professional journalism product. The public voice for the Bondy Blog is a product that can be delivered to the mainstream media as well as a force that can be used to expand perspectives included in the news. While by most accounts Bondy Blog is seen as an incredible resource, Hamid's defensiveness signals a still underdeveloped idea about what the public's role ought to be.

NewsTrust and NewsCred

Social news sites, rather than seeing the public as reporters or sources, position the public primarily in the roles traditionally reserved for editors as aggregators, evaluators, and gatekeepers. First-generation of social news sites like Digg, Reddit, StumbleUpon, and FriendFeed rely entirely on user-aggregated and user-ranked stories to make up the content of their sites, granting the users the role of gatekeeper. They depend on the wisdom of the crowd and facilitate groups of individuals to collectively determine the value or importance of content disseminated through the community. The users are given the editorial power to influence the visibility of content. Despite the popularity of these sites, critics question the quality of their information and the fairness of a system that allows users to "bury" stories simply because they don't agree with them.

Sites like NewsTrust sponsored by the MacArthur Foundation and NewsCred, an international startup based in Geneva and Stockholm, have launched a second generation of social news sites that aggregate and rate stories based on quality, not just popularity. Users' news-based credibility ratings are averaged across all users to determine the trustworthiness of each article, author, and publication. Based on these ratings the sites use algorithms to promote the stories with the highest quality rating. The goal is not only to improve the aggregation process in order bring together high-quality news items but also to engage the community of readers in critically assessing the material, therefore becoming more engaged with it.

NewsTrust created a guide to news literacy meant to help reviewers on their site "make sense of all this digital noise," and inviting them to "think like a journalist" in order to learn to "distinguish news from opinion, become familiar with journalism principles and ethics, and sharpen your critical judgment." The guide outlines four "distinct traits" of reporters that can be used as a guide to rating the quality of their work. Good journalists, according to the NewsTrust guidelines: "1. *Doubt* – they have a healthy skepticism. 2. *Detect* – they have a 'nose for news.' 3.

Discern – they place a priority on fairness, balance and objectivity.
4. *Demand* – they focus on free access to information and freedom of speech" (Bujeja 2009). NewsTrust is based on the idea that by assessing journalism by this set of criteria, the public together with professional members of the site will serve as an aggregator of high-quality journalism and a watchdog of poor-quality journalism.

Le Monde blogger Francis Pisani wrote:

> Rating with multiple criteria has a curious effect: at first, you're encouraged to read the article more carefully. And when it's time to rate the article, you feel an irresistible need to take a second look at certain sections, to make sure that your verdict will be correct. This invites a more attentive and critical review, making us better readers. And this is one of NewsTrust's central objectives. (Romero 2007)

On NewsCred, every article aggregated on the site from a collection of pre-approved top news and blog sources can be either "credited" or "discredited" and then ranked for "credibility." On NewsTrust the scoring of credibility is more comprehensive: stories are rated on a 1 to 5 star scale in eleven categories, including fairness, balance, context, importance, style, and trust. The ratings are then combined and averaged for an overall rating on the story that, in theory, reflects all of those factors. On both sites, users can comment on stories and add additional information and sources.

These new social news-filtering sites combine traditional and emergent news practices and values. News judgment is taken out of the hands of traditional gatekeepers – editors – and given to the public while at the same time promoting the traditional values of accuracy, fairness, and credibility. These sites aim to distinguish quality content, revive public trust in news, and to some extent educate the public in new ways of relating to the media environment. Members of the public are, thus, seen as a resource in the process of the assessment and curation of stories and information, and as students in the process of learning to critically evaluate news products. Technologies that combine user and algorithmic ranking to identify and promote quality stories will likely help shape the future of news, simultaneously teaching new media news literacy by inviting users to assess content based on quality, and by inspiring the creation of higher quality work. The next chapter delves more deeply into the ways people are using new technologies to forge new opportunities to be involved in the creation, distribution and editing of news.

Opening Access

The cases discussed in this chapter are not meant to represent all news experiments in public involvement; they were chosen because they are each driven by distinct views of the public. Each one illustrates an emergent role for the public and demonstrates that perceptions of the public are not given or natural but socially constructed. These experiments involving the former audience feed the narrative of newly empowered publics and, upon closer examination, also demonstrate the ways in which the nature and extent of the publics' involvement, at least in the most high-profile and traditional-media-driven experiments explored in this chapter, is still largely shaped by news professionals and enduring notions of professional authority.

The BBC sees members of the public as helpers, using them as a resource, eliciting their help as eyewitnesses and information gatherers while keeping tight control on how that content is integrated into the professional BBC-brand news product. OTB played on "citizen journalists'" distinct lack of professional training in order to generate fresh perspectives and push the boundaries of professional journalism while at the same time drawing on the norms and practices of traditional journalism, not least in the enduring control professional editors had over content. Bondy Blog created a conduit of hard-to-access hyperlocal content by turning members of the public into journalists and exploiting their expertise as members of banlieue communities. The content then became a product to deliver to the mainstream media as well as a force to expand perspectives included in the news. And finally first-generation social news sites like Digg construct the public as aggregator while the more quality-minded NewsTrust facilitated public curation of news content by educating members of the public on the nuances of what makes for quality journalism, and by implementing rating systems that allow members to act as editors – promoting stories based on their quality and importance.

The distinct but sometimes overlapping branches of new perceptions of the public illustrated here – as helper, source, reporter, instigator, aggregator, evaluator, and curator – are also shaped by a combination of new communication tools and networks and by market demand. Economic strain has made offering free content and providing a platform for participation by users essential components of networked era news outlets and platforms. And a decline in readership and trust has influenced decisions to engage readers in new ways. Facilitating participation is both a form of marketing and a way to encourage civic engagement, or, as news and activist media scholar Chris Atton sees it, "to add a contemporary sheen to dominant practices, thus demonstrating that established news organizations are sensitive to popular cultural change" (2009: 141).

While professional news organizations have in some cases succeeded in their attempts to leverage public participation to their advantage, this participation presents fundamental challenges to professional news organizations, challenges that won't likely go away by the incorporation of this content into the routines of professional journalism. The most significant change is that the central role of professionalism is receding, which offers the possibility of deliberation and pluralization of content by opening access to people and points of view traditionally excluded, and which changes how truth claims are made. "Truth" as the exclusive domain of authorities and the journalists who use them as sources is challenged and making room for communication created by the public based on storytelling, exchange, and perspectives that have been traditionally excluded. To Atton this means that "the political economy of the news industry today is in a very real sense doing more to shuffle and in some ways open up access than any degree of boycott or other overt challenge" (2009: 144). We see examples of this especially in Bondy Blog, which offers lived experience of banlieue youth – using everyday people as sources, asking questions about issues of local import to politicians, critiquing and making themselves visible in a media landscape that has made them invisible, and broadening the coverage of the 2005 riots as well as related issues such as discrimination, unemployment, police harassment, and immigration. This is also evident at OTB, which generated alternative campaign narratives by highlighting non-media professionals' view of candidates and issues. The significance of this involvement goes beyond the quality and diversity of content to a change in perception about what news is and what it does. As more and more people are involved in the newsmaking process, and as that process becomes a news topic in and of itself with coverage of coverage a staple of news cycles, the more widespread the consciousness of reality construction as an aspect of news production will become. News is no longer naturalized. The "underlying arbitrariness" of the news, as media scholar Nicolas Couldry (2003) puts it, is no longer obscured by the symbolic power of its representations, thus opening it up to increased scrutiny and criticism.

Yet while the barriers that formerly separated the sources, reporters, and audiences are dissolving, there are still rigid, distinct lines. OTB was ghettoized at the Huffington Post. Its citizen-generated content was considered by some of the news section editors to be "fluffier" than the rest of the sites' news content. And the content was edited and fact-checked by OTB editors (John Tomasic, unpublished interview with author 2008). *L'Hebdo* professional editors think of themselves as trainers and, in order to teach and to elevate the quality of content, they edited and fact-checked the work of Bondy bloggers. And at the BBC, the UGC Hub is contentious among some of its reporters and editors whose professionalism has long rested on their access to bureaucratically credible sources and on keeping their distance from their audiences.

Despite the close reins media outlets keep on their own content, the reality is that news production has raced beyond industry control. Corporate news will not vanish any time soon but will continue to decrease in its dominance over the social dialogue as emerging news models fulfill social needs that have been neglected by the model that constructs members of the public as passive consumers of news. The mainstream news industry is poaching new-style digital news products, practices and, at times, values in order to remain relevant – hiring and training bloggers, using information and sources culled from the web to inform their stories, eliciting the local perspectives of their readers. We can see evidence of this already in the ways mainstream journalists are mimicking the styles of citizen journalism and amateurs who in turn are modeling the voice, tone, and news values of the pros. And on the other hand, the discourse of these alternative forms – citizen journalists and gatekeepers, in the case of social news sites – is still largely influenced not only by frames and agendas set by the national and international mainstream media but also by the norms and practices of traditional journalism.

This influence, however, is not enough to quell critics who equate the receding authority and relevance of the professional journalism industry, and the economic security that it used to enjoy, with the demise of journalism itself. The next two chapters address some of the technological and cultural shifts in news and argue that these shifts are making room for new forms of journalism, some of which can and will more directly involve the public.

Notes

1 Creative Commons (http://creativecommons.org/) is a nonprofit organization that provides free licenses that allow creators to tailor the copyright permissions associated with their content. The concluding chapter includes a discussion of the role of copyright reform efforts like this one in the future of the news landscape.

2 Its programming reaches roughly 275 million people in thirty-three languages in 200 countries, and since the 1920s the BBC has been the dominant broadcast network in the U.K.

3 The controversy surrounding the BBC reached a peak recently with the Hutton inquiry and subsequent report in response to the 2003 death of Dr. David Kelly, a Ministry of Defence employee, after he had been named as the source of quotes used by a BBC journalist. The quotes had been the basis of news reports claiming that Tony Blair and his staff had intentionally exaggerated the threat of Weapons of Mass Destruction in the "September Dossier," a government report gauging the threat of Iraq. The government was eventually

cleared of wrongdoing but the BBC was strongly criticized, leading to the resignation of the BBC's chairman and director-general.

References

Anderson, K. (2009) "Media140: Twitter and Covering the US Elections," May 25. http://strange.corante.com/2009/05/25/media140-twitter-and-covering-the-us-elections

Arendt, H. (1968) *Men in Dark Times*. New York: Harcourt, Brace & World, Inc.

Atton, C. (2009) "Why Alternative Journalism Matters." *Journalism: Theory, Practice and Criticism* 10:3, 283–5.

BBC (2008) "Sharia Law in UK is 'Unavoidable'," February 7. http://news.bbc.co.uk/2/hi/uk_news/7232661.stm

BBC (2008/9) Statements of Programme Policy. http://www.bbc.co.uk/about thebbc/statements2008/

Boczkowski, P.J. (2005) *Digitizing the News*. Cambridge, MA: MIT Press.

Born, G. (2002) "Reflexivity and Ambivalence: Culture, Creativity and Government in the BBC." *Journal for Cultural Research* 6:1–2, 65–90.

Bujeja, M. (2009) "Think Like a Journalist: A New Literacy Guide from NewsTrust." NewsTrust. http://newstrust.net/guides/

Carey, J. (1987) "The Press and Public Discourse." *The Center Magazine*, March/April, 4–16.

Case, T. (1994) "Public Journalism Denounced." *Editor and Publisher*, November 12, 14–15.

Castells, M. (1997) *The Power of Identity*. Oxford: Blackwell Publishers.

Clark, J. & Aufderheide, P. (2009) "Public Media 2.0: Dynamic, Engaged Publics." http://www.centerforsocialmedia.org/future-public-media/documents/ white-papers/public-media-20-dynamic-engaged-publics

Cleaver, H. (1998a) "The Zapatistas and the Electronic Fabric of Struggle." In: J. Holloway & E. Pelaez (eds), *Zapatista! Reinventing Revolution in Mexico*. Chicago: Pluto Publishing.

Cleaver, H. (1998b) "The Zapatista Effect: The Internet and the Rise of an Alternative Political Fabric." http://libcom.org/library/zapatista-effect-cleaver

Congdon, T., Davies, G., & Graham, A. (1992) *Paying for Broadcasting*. London: Routledge.

Couldry, N. (2003) "Media Meta-Capital: Extending the Range of Bourdieu's Field Theory." *Theory and Society* 32, 653–77.

Dewey, J. (1922) "Public Opinion." *The New Republic*, May 3.

Echchaibi, N. (2009) "From the Margins to the Center: New Media and the Case of Bondy Blog in France." In: A. Russell & N. Echchaibi (eds), *International Blogging*. New York: Peter Lang.

Fallows, J. (1997) *Breaking the News: How the Media Undermine American Democracy*. New York: Vintage.

Felouzis G., Liot F., & Perroton J. (2005) *L'apartheid scolaire: Enquête sur la ségrégation ethnique dans les collèges*. Paris: Éditions du Seuil.

Frederick, H.H. (1992) "Computer Communications in Cross-Border Coalition Building." *Gazette: The International Journal for Mass Communication Studies* 50:2–3, 217–41.

Froehling, O. (1997) "The Cyberspace War of Ink and Internet in Chiapas, Mexico." *Geographical Review* 87:2, 291–307.

Goodin, E. (2007) "Networks Scour Facebook." *National Journal*, April 17. http://hotlineoncall.nationaljournal.com/archives/2007/04/networks_scour.php

Gillmor, D. (2004) *We the Media*. Sebastopol, CA: O'Reilly Media.

Glasser, T. (1999) *The Idea of Public Journalism*. New York: Guilford Press.

Glasser, T. (1984) "Objectivity Precludes Responsibility." *The Quill*, February, 13–16.

Hermida, A. (2008) "User-Generated Content as a Form of Newsgathering." Reportr.net, November 1. http://www.reportr.net/2008/11/01/user-generated-content-as-a-form-of-newsgathering/

Hermida, A. (2009) "The Blogging BBC: Journalism Blogs at 'the World's Most Trusted News Organization'." *Journalism Practice* 3:3, 1–17.

Hermida, A. (2010) "E-Democracy Remixed: Learning from the BBC's Action Network and the Shift from a Static Commons to a Participatory Multiplex." *Journal of eDemocracy* 2:2, 119–30.

Horrock, P. (2008) "Value of Citizen Journalism." BBC: The Editors, January 7. http://www.bbc.co.uk/blogs/theeditors/2008/01/value_of_citizen_journalism.html

Huffington, A. & Rosen, J. (2008) "Thanks to the People who Worked on Off the Bus."

Huffington Post, November. http://www.huffingtonpost.com/arianna-huffing-ton-and-jay-rosen/thanks-to-the-people-who-_b_144476.html

Huynh, K. (2007) "Paul ou la révélation de banlieues." Bondy Blog, October 30. http://20minutes.bondyblog.fr/news/paul-ou-la-revelation-des-banlieues

Johnson, B. & Clarke, C. (2007) "America's First User-Generated Confession." *Guardian*, April 23. http://www.guardian.co.uk/media/2007/apr/23/monday mediasection.facebook

Jouvenal, J. & Koppelman, A. (2008) "Vanity Fair Piece about Bill Clinton Sparks Controversy." Salon.com, June 3. http://www.salon.com/news/politics/war_room/2008/06/03/vf_clinton/print.html

Knudson, J.W. (1998) "Rebellion in Chiapas: Insurrection by Internet and Public Relations." *Media, Culture & Society* 20:3, 507–18.

Lippmann W. (1922) *Public Opinion*. New York: The Free Press.

Michel, A. (2009) "Get Off the Bus: The Future of Pro–Am Journalism."

Columbia Journalism Review, March/April. http://www.cjr.org/feature/get_off_the_bus.php

Netanel, N. (2002) "The Commercial Mass Media's Continuing Fourth Estate Role." In: N. Netanel & N. Elkin-Koren (eds), *The Commodification of Information*. London: Kluwer Law International.

Newseum Website (2008) "Newseum in the News," October 28. http://www.newseum.org/press-info/newseum-in-the-news/index.html

Poynter (2009) *"New York Times'* Policy on Facebook and Other Social Networking Sites," January 19. http://mountainrunner.us/2009/0S/nyt_facebook_policy.html.

Remnick, D. (1996) "Scoop." *The New Yorker*, January 29.

Romero, L. (2007) "What the Press Says about NewsTrust." Net[2], April 15. http://www.netsquared.org/blog/leo-romero/what-press-says-about-newstrust

Rosen, J. (2006a) "The People Formerly Known as the Audience." PressThink, June 27. http://journalism.nyu.edu/pubzone/weblogs/pressthink/2006/06/27/ppl_frmr.html

Rosen, J. (2006b) "Introducing Newsassignment.net." PressThink, July 25. http://journalism.nyu.edu/pubzone/weblogs/pressthink/2006/07/25/nadn_qa.html

Rosen, J. (2008) "When Mayhill Fowler Met Bill Clinton at the Rope Line." PressThink, June 9. http://journalism.nyu.edu/pubzone/weblogs/pressthink/2008/06/09/fowler_clinton_p.html

Russell, A. (2005) "Zapatista Myths: Exploring a Network Identity." *New Media and Society* 7:4, 559–77.

Steinberg, J. (2008) "For New Journalists, All Bets but Not Mikes, are Off." *New York Times*, June 8. http://www.nytimes.com/2008/06/08/weekinreview/08steinberg.html

Stelter, B. (2010) "Honoring Citizen Journalists." *New York Times*, February 21. http://www.nytimes.com/2010/02/22/business/media/22polk.html

Tate, R (2010) "Cell-Phone 'Neda' Cameraman wins Polk Award." Gawker, February 16. http://gawker.com/5473153/cell+phone-neda-cameraman-wins-polk-award

Tomasic, J. (2009) "Moreen Dowd: Parasitic Blogger." Colorado Independent, May 18. http://coloradoindependent.com/29210/maureen-dowd-parasitic-blogger

Tompkins, A. (2007) "Students Tell Va. Tech Story Through Cell Video, Blogs, Forums," April 17. http://www.poynter.org/column.asp?id=2&aid=121541

3

From Personalization to Socialization

[T]he user decides what's important.
The horror.

J.D. Lasica (2002)

In 1995, Massachusetts Institute of Technology Media Lab founder Nicholas Negroponte described his vision of a coming internet-based news environment more personalized and less controlled by the mass-market tastes, where consumers not editors or news anchors increasingly came to decide what was news. It seemed typically Negroponte, a techno-optimistic image of a world where the blow-dried deadening power of soundbite broadcast news faded, where individualized and engaged newsgathering replaced mere watching or reading.

> Instead of reading what other people think is news and what other people justify as worthy of the space it takes, being digital will change the economic model of news selection, make your interests take a bigger role, and, in fact use pieces from the cutting room floor that did not make the cut on popular demand. (Negroponte 1995: 153)

Just over a decade later, *Wired Magazine* cofounder Chris Anderson (2006) outlined the power of what he called the long tail, a phenomenon that he described as occurring across cultural industries. Anderson described how catering to people's niche interests was becoming a profitable business model in the networked era. Distributors like Amazon increasingly make profits

71

not only from the "short head" of their product – a small number of bestsellers – but also from the "long tail" – a wide variety of niche products with small circulation. Tailoring to the specialized interest of news publics through a variety of technologies has been a key feature of online news since its early days. The long tail has been celebrated for bringing new voices and perspective into the public conversation on events (Gillmor 2004). It has also elicited anxiety among those concerned that by not receiving the same news, or experiencing the same media events, members of the public are no longer bound by a common mediated experience (Sunstein 2002). Personalized news is one of the factors upending the mass-media news industry business model, which is built on attracting large audiences to sell to advertisers.

The 1990s vision of personalized news, however, has come only partly to life as the network era has evolved. There has been a turn in direction from news personalization to news socialization. Part of that has to do with the cultural contexts in which technologies are developing and being taken up by the former audience. Indeed, the shape of communications technologies, like all technologies, is the result of particular historical and cultural realities. James Carey (1998), writing in response to techno-determinist or at least techno-determinist-leaning analysts like Negroponte, said that technology is not "something lying about in the bosom of nature that we just happen to be smart enough to discover." He said analysts had to strive to "re-embed" technology with culture. What was new about new technology as the network era dawned? What was it about journalism culture, the producers and the publics, that gave the early networked era its shape and set it off in one direction or another?

This chapter explores these questions by reviewing early online news experiments and the subsequent emergence of the so-called "Web 2.0" technologies and their support of an increasingly sophisticated infrastructure for social exchange. The changes in habits of news producer and of networked publics are demonstrated in the roll-out of these tools during the December 2009 United Nations Summit on Climate Change (COP15). The chapter ultimately argues that there has been a shift from personalization to socialization of news, and that with this shift comes new potential for accountability journalism as well as for new forms of journalism that facilitate deliberation and pluralism.

Customizing News: From the Daily Me to the Daily We

For Negroponte and Anderson and many other web visionaries, the utopian rhetoric hinged on the promise that technologies would facilitate the creation and distribution of information free of the taste-making, agenda-setting hierarchies of media industry executives. Early attempts at catering to individual tastes, however, did not send people down the "long tail" to access content absent from the mainstream. Instead, people were encouraged mostly to customize mainstream content, which of course is material spun from the taste-making, agenda-setting hierarchies of media industry executives.

One of the first customized personal news services was Freshman Fishwrap, a MIT Media Lab class project in 1993. The assignment was to design a personalized news system for incoming freshmen so they could easily access the news from their hometowns. Students developed a program that created a customized package of news each day according to user zip codes and topics of interest. Fishwrap also allowed subscribers to add topics and tailored content based on what reader histories built up from each day's reading. The experiment caught on quickly and eventually won roughly 700 users in the wider MIT community. It also inspired a steady stream of experimentation with news customization. Pointcast, for example, launched their personalized news software in 1996, which used so-called "SmartScreen" technology to bring up news like a screensaver when computers went idle, freeze the screen on stories of interest, and send the full text to a website where the user could access it. Pointcast bombed, however, partly because it was a bandwidth hog in the age of the dialup modem and was banned in places where it clogged internet "tubes" (Meyer 2006).

73

Around the same time, web portals such as MyYahoo and MyExcite launched personalization services that allowed users to choose their favorite news topics for display. Beginning in the late nineties, mainstream news organizations began offering personalized news service modeled on internet portals. Most let users select from customized news categories and geographic regions. The online arms of network television stations offered users the option of pulling information from local TV affiliate stations to access news, weather, and sports.

Despite the fact that these services offered only mainstream news content, author and social media expert J.D. Lasica saw the trend toward personalization as transformative. In 2002 he wrote:

> No trend threatens the guardians of old media more than personalization. The very notion challenges the philosophical underpinnings of traditional media: We, the gatekeepers, gather the news and tell you what's important. Under this chiseled-in-stone setup, editors sort through and rank the news, controlling everything from the assignment of stories to their tone, slant and prominence on the page.
>
> Personalized news reduces the role of editors in the news equation. The reporter writes the story, the copy editor (if there is one) edits it, another person indexes it for easy retrieval, and the user decides what's important.
>
> The horror.

In March 2000, when the economic bubble floating the internet entrepreneurial boom burst, personalization was still a main idea driving thinking about online news. The rhetoric, though, was forced to change. Slowly the digerati began talking about a "Web 2.0," a new and improved post-bubble internet culture. The idea gained traction in part, surely, because it put distance between new ideas of digital life and old ideas of digital life – or at least between the new ideas and the recently new discredited ideas associated with the culture of a million-and-one frothy light dot-com startups. The Web 2.0 reframing revived people's confidence in online business ventures but more importantly it shifted the focus from the personal to the social. Social networking – that is, leveraging connected communities online for information gathering and aggregation – became a new guiding concept. The news industry, however, didn't take up that concept; it didn't join with the digerati in wading back into internet-land. Instead, it beat a retreat from the internet, appearing in retrospect to breathe a collective sigh of relief and return to offline business as usual for a decade, stalling its involvement in building the future news environment and creating more space for web developers and entrepreneurs to move in (Kevin Anderson, unpublished interview with author 2008).

Transformative Technologies and Practices

In that decade, however, shifts in technology and audience expectation would dramatically change the nature of journalism. According to a Center for Social Media report, low-cost and easy-to-use digital tools combined with widely accessible online and mobile distribution networks "have made it possible for everyone to be not only a consumer of media but also a creator, to not be only a receiver but a selector, recommender, participant or curator" (Aufderheide et al. 2009: 3). It's the decade where we shifted from mass audience members to networked users.

Web 2.0 is facilitated through second-generation technology aimed at harnessing collective intelligence, mainly web-based tools and platforms such as blogs and social networking sites through which users collaborate and share information and, increasingly, harness the "long tail" of news media material. Originally conceived to revive ailing internet industries, the long-tail business model is increasingly driving emergent journalism practices and news consumer habits. Blogs, social networks, hackable platforms, and mobile devices decentralize networks of communication and exchange. Yochai Benkler describes the result as a

flourishing nonmarket sector of information, knowledge, and cultural production, based in the networked environment, and applied to anything the many individuals connected to it can imagine. Its outputs, in turn are not treated as exclusive property; they are instead subject to an increasingly robust ethic of open sharing, open for all others to build on, extend, and make their own. (2006: 6–7)

Blogs

There were no blogs until there were blogs and then suddenly they were uncountable. The urge was met and fostered by the rise of blogging platforms. Before free and easy to use sites like Blogger and LiveJournal, getting up and running on the web meant writing or changing code manually. Blogging made the web writable. Pyra labs released Blogger (later acquired by Google) in 1999. It was the first content management system that allowed people with no technical skills to create and update websites. Blogs replaced email lists and personal websites as vehicles for exchanging ideas and information. Rebecca Blood (2000), early blogger and chronicler of the blogging phenomenon, describes the transformation that blogs brought about:

> The promise of the web was that everyone could publish, that a thousand voices could flourish, communicate, connect. The truth was that only those people who knew how to code a web page could make their voices heard. Blogger, Pitas, and all the rest have given people with little or no knowledge of HTML the ability to publish: to pontificate, remember, dream, and argue in public, as easily as they send an instant message.

Although blogs could link to one another and to other web content, they did not really become web-conversational until the development of RSS feeds and permalinks. RSS ("Really Simple Syndication") allowed the web to "go live," by making it possible to subscribe to all your favorite sites and know the moment they've been updated. Permalinks ensured that content was accessible and reliably linked to or from and cited by outside sources.

According to Tim O'Reilly, founder and C.E.O. of O'Reilly Media, which publishes some of the most influential books and online content on emergent technologies: "While Mainstream media may see individual blogs as competitors, what is really unnerving is that the competition is with the blogosphere as a

76

whole. This is not just a competition between sites but a competition between business models" (2005: 10). By new model, he means Web 2.0. O'Reilly sees the blogosphere and the business model it supposedly represents as having an advantage over traditional new models because it delivers a "rich user experience" that centers on collaboration. It creates software that lives on the network and gets better the more people use it, and it sees users providing their own data and services in forms that encourage remixing by other users.

Blogging is a social practice that came to augment professional news forms and pressure news organizations from both inside and outside newsrooms. One of the most visible and controversial roles of the blogosphere, in an early iteration at least, was the way it overlapped with and repurposed mainstream media. An early example often cited as evidence of the power of the blogosphere to influence the agenda of the mainstream media came in 2002 when bloggers exposed racist comments made by Majority Senate leader Trent Lott, who ultimately resigned as a result. While at a birthday party for Senator Strom Thurmond, who ran for president in 1948 on a racial segregationist platform, Lott made a public statement that the United States would have been better off had Thurmond been elected president. Journalists present at the party buried the quote but bloggers circulated it widely with added information they had dug up about past racially charged comments made by Lott. Mainstream news organizations were then forced to pick the story back up. The information flow went back and forth.

The exchange only increased. Bloggers everywhere serve as real-time fact-checkers and critics of the news of the day. By the end of 2004, blogs had become a key part of online news culture, and by the end of the decade, many bloggers became essential reading for members of the media and the public, bloggers with different political views and different approaches to the medium, like Markos Moulistas, Glenn Greenwald, Eric Erickson, and Matt Drudge (Bruns 2005: 18). These bloggers had developed their own personal news brand, picking up tips, building sources, and breaking stories. Mainstream media outlets eventually began hiring news blogosphere stars. What's more, as mentioned above, bloggers came to increasingly work together, building stories at their individual blogs by linking to one another and adding new information to push breaking news or investigative pieces forward, but also by joining group-blogs, like progressive politics blogsite DailyKos, to set up de facto news outlets. Something the mainstream traditional news media didn't seem to realize was that, in the end, it was merely a question of numbers. Because anyone with access to an internet connection could become a blogger, they came to outnumber journalists exponentially and without incurring any overheads) for a company to generate profits to pay. Surveys by the Pew Internet & American Life Project in 2004 reported that 8 million American adults had created blogs, and that blog readership jumped 58 percent in 2004 to 27 percent of all internet users (Rainie 2005).

By 2010, reporter blogs had become a staple among newspaper and broadcast networks looking to heighten reader engagement and loyalty. Some news outlets, like the *Houston Chronicle* and the London *Guardian*, provide platforms for readers to blog on in hopes of creating communities around their product. Others, like the BBC and the *New York Times*, use blogs to extend and deepen coverage with reader input or by posting updates and to field reader questions and comments. According to *New York Times* City Room Blog Editor Jennifer 8. Lee, blogs have contributed to a shift in the relationship between audience and journalists at the *New York Times*. After the Jayson Blair scandal,[1] for example, it opened up lines of communication between the *New York Times* and wary readers who could fact-check dubious reporting. The paper's staff also mined readers for story ideas and content. Lee said the paper's blogs contributed to the evolution of writing styles to reflect the dominant aesthetic of the web. *New York Times* writers, she said, wrote less formally, with more intimacy and immediacy on their blogs (unpublished interview with author 2009).

The adoption of blogs in mainstream newsrooms has not been without controversy. Some argue that blogs challenge the norms and practice of the profession, including non-partisanship and the gatekeeping role (Singer 2001). Many suggest that blogs are inherently subjective and thus necessarily challenge the norms of objectivity. In fact several reporters have been forced by editors to stop blogging because it was seen as not impartial or otherwise compromising to the perceived quality of the news organization's product (Allan 2006). Even so, many professional journalists maintain blogs for expressing experiences and ideas that do not conform to the conventions of traditional news stories. Some argue that news organizations may be more interested in containing and directing the blogging phenomenon than in facilitating democratic participation (Lowrey 2006: 493), and that while journalists engage in new forms of writing in blogs, they are also attempting to recapture journalistic authority online (Robinson 2006). Perhaps satirical newsman Jon Stewart reflected this view best when he described mainstream media blogs as "giving voice to the already voiced."

Social Networks

Early online communities such as The Well (1985), Geocities (1994), and Tripod (1995) served as social network sites. Users interacted in chatrooms and at personal homepages published with tools made available through the sites. Later social networking sites such as Facebook and MySpace allow people to create profiles, connect with other users, and view overlapping lists of network members (Boyd & Ellison 2007). The technology evolved but so did the organizational logic. Later social networks were organized primarily around people not interests. Early public online communities, discussion forums and Usenets, were structured by topics or according to topical hierarchies. Social network sites are structured as personal (or "egocentric") networks, with the individual at the center of their own community. This more accurately mirrors unmediated social structures, where "the world is composed of networks not groups" (Wellman 1988: 37). Many news organizations have shifted their personalization services based on topics of interest to social network platforms organized around people. The *New York Times* stopped advertising and linking to its early networking site MyTimes in December 2009 two years after it launched. MyTimes allowed readers to organize content from any web source and directly from lists of favorite sources provided by *New York Times* writers. It offered users a number of subject widgets: that is, stand-alone applications that can be embedded into other sites, a sort of portable tiny icons for different topics. There were the *New York Times* crossword, photos, select articles, movie showtimes, mortgage rates, weather, and stocks quotes. In 2010, the paper began promoting TimesPeople, a platform that functions more like Facebook or MySpace in that it allows users to link to other people, creating communities of online "friends" who point one another to material.

News organizations aren't just trying to build branded communities of users, though; they're also trying to use social networking to connect with the public. Facebook, according to web analytics company Alexa, is the second-most heavily trafficked site globally, second only to Google. As of April 2010, Facebook reports it has more than 400 million active users. According to a World Association of Newspapers (2007) study of young people's news habits from ten different countries, participants listed "discussion with friends" as their top source for news and information – higher than television and print news. The authors of the study suggest that the best strategy is for news organizations to insert themselves into these new social networks. Many are doing just that. Journalists began posting stories and updates on Facebook and Twitter to promote their work. Most news sites now provide widgets that can be downloaded to a reader's personal browser or website. Networked publics linked through other online communities use social bookmarking and aggregation tools like Digg, Netvibes, StumbleUpon, and Reddit to embed links and vote for favorites in order to drive them up the "must view" hierarchy.

According to a 2010 Pew Internet and American Life Project, 30 percent of internet users get news from friends, journalists, or news organizations they follow on social networking sites. Adding that to the fact that nearly three-quarters of online teens and young adults use social network sites (Lenhart et al. 2010), news industry professionals recognize social networking sites as an essential journalism platform. James Brady, executive editor of washingtonpost.com, says he uses social media to draw in young readers: "The one thing that gets lost in all the automation and search engine gaming algorithms is that people want to know what their friends think and what people respect. One way to get content in front of you is to have your friends recommend it; that's a social filtering of news" (as quoted in Emmett 2009).

By 2010, the micro-blogging platform Twitter became perhaps the ultimate social networking tool. Members post or "tweet" short notes – no more than 140 typed characters – for the benefit of their Twitter "followers," linking to sites all over the web and posting photos and reporting witnessed events large and small. Twitter has become a staple tool for journalists, who use it not just to report and repost their stories, but also to break stories and disseminate pieces for immediate discussion. Because Twitter is an open platform, people can develop tools to help them tailor it to their needs, tweaking it to allow them to post, read, aggregate, and search content in ways most convenient to them. Unlike broadcast or print outlets, Twitter fosters conversation by encouraging discussion and feedback, allowing journalists to build a rapport with readers and gauge public opinion. It also makes the public feel more connected to the news by facilitating discussion about news events as they unfold.

Hackable Platforms

Open-source web tools and applications are becoming increasingly customizable. Media makers can tailor their platforms, sharing tips across a broad community of developers, and users can pick and choose how they will interact with content. Widgets allow news publics to bring the news to where they are. In 2007, for example, the BBC launched a redesign of the site that allows the user to build their own front pages, in effect, by moving their favorite content from within the BBC to the front page. The design aimed to make content more accessible, rather than making the page a necessary one-stop destination. Richard Titus (2007), head of user experience and design at the BBC, explained:

> From a conceptual point of view, the widgetization adopted by Facebook, iGoogle and netvibes weighed strongly on our initial

thinking. We wanted to build the foundation and DNA of the new site in line with the ongoing trend and evolution of the Internet towards dynamically generated and syndicatable content through technologies like RSS, atom and xml.

Some of the most innovative journalists are creating sharable databases and allowing their software to be reprogrammed by outside developers through Application Programming Interface (API). An API is like a set of building blocks with specific language describing what the blocks are, but not specifically how you should use them. They are means by which outside developers can access data for use in other applications, interfaces, and mashups. Facebook APIs allow developers to integrate Facebook into an existing site, build Facebook iPhone apps, or create an application that runs in Facebook. Google Maps APIs let you embed and manipulate Google Maps in your own version of the web, fitted with your favorite sites and material.

In October 2008 the *New York Times* released its first API, the Campaign Finance API, which allowed users to retrieve contribution and expenditure data based on U.S. Federal Election Commission filings. *New York Times* developers organized public campaign finance data from a variety of sources into aggregates that answer most campaign finance questions. In their description of the service to their readers, they wrote that "Instead of poring over monthly filings or searching a disclosure database, you can use the Times Campaign Finance API to quickly retrieve totals for a particular candidate, see aggregates by ZIP code or state, or get details on a particular donor" (API Documentation and Tools 2010).

Derek Willis, newsroom developer at the *New York Times*, said these applications were built in order to illuminate existing stories. He believes that people should be exposed to raw data, but that sharing this kind of unadorned information with the public and other journalists goes against the central impulses of traditional journalistic practice. "There is a natural tendency to keep information and data to ourselves because of competition and the desire to keep it close until we are ready. Some would say this is because we don't want to surrender authority" (unpublished interview with author 2009).

Journalist and technology innovator Adrian Holovaty (2006) believes journalists need to move beyond the role of information gathers and storywriters: "So much of what local journalists collect day-to-day is structured information: the type of information that can be sliced-and-diced, in an automated fashion, by computers." Holovaty's hyperlocal news site Everyblock, launched with support from a Knight Foundation News Challenge Grant and acquired in 2009 by MSNBC, filters news by location so you can get information about your city, your neighborhood, or your block. In 2009, Everyblock covered fifteen U.S. cities, collecting already existing information and records from government agencies and officials, journalists, businesses, and the public. It creates geographic filters or news feeds that allow users to get a rich vein of hyperlocal specific consumer, crime, housing information, and more on neighborhoods that at least theoretically is being constantly updated.

Another innovative data-driven journalism platform, the Ujima Project, collects data on African government and NGO spending and makes it accessible to anyone seeking access to information not readily available in many African countries, partly owing to a lack of freedom of information laws. The project was founded in 2009 by Investigative Reporters and Editors (IRE), and the nonprofit Great Lakes Media Institute. Ujima was developed and is maintained by AppFrica, a Kampala-based software development firm in Uganda. The project functions as a sort of mechanism of reverse transparency by compiling information from government webpages and other sites on the web and offline information from documents that are manually entered, making it easily accessible and searchable. All of the raw data will soon be available via an API and the project has just launched a mobile app to make the data accessible via Nokia phones. This allows journalists and others to track details about, for example, what a particular NGO is doing, or how much money a particular African government is spending to influence policy in the United States or the European Union.

Mobile News

Mobile devices are increasingly being used to both access news and information and to create and circulate news-related content, especially in developing countries where cell phones are ubiquitous. SMS or text message-based updates on issues and breaking events, election monitoring, snapshots of breaking news, and live audio or video streaming are all helping to shape news coverage. Pew estimates that by 2020 mobile devices will be the primary tool for connecting to the internet (Rainie & Anderson 2008). In Asia and Europe, mobile devices are already powerful tools for both producing and consuming text, audio, photo, and video content. As Global Positioning System-enabled mobile devices like Apple's iPhone and Google's Nexus One allow users to access and upload geographically relevant content, a new set of hyperlocal news platforms like Everyblock are being enabled. Maps are also becoming a common interface for news, video, and data. According to Pew, 80 percent of American adults have cell phones today and 37 percent of those Americans use their phones to surf the web. One quarter of all Americans say they consume some form of news via cell phone today. That amounts to 33 percent of cell phone owners (Purcell et al. 2010). Derek Willis predicts that the most significant change in journalism over the next decade will be the impact of mobile devices on how journalism gets done:

> If you think of the way most journalism is done now, that process (save for radio) was never designed for a mobile device with real capabilities. A lot of the people who will consume journalism ten years from now will do so on mobile devices, and a lot of those people will be relatively early in their news consumption habits. We have to figure out how and where to meet them, and keep them around. (Unpublished interview with author 2010)

Media Climate: Case Study

All of the above-described emergent tools and practices were manifest in online coverage of the December 2009 UN Climate

Summit (COP15), as was the enduring presence of traditional national media. The stark contrast between the online and offline media environment came to life to me while doing research as part of MediaClimate, a global study of news coverage of the Climate Summit aimed at gauging and comparing coverage from eighteen countries around the world. I was charged with analyzing the coverage in the news pages of the *New York Times* and *USA Today*. What I found there was significantly different than the coverage I found online, including work at the websites of these same two news outlets. The websites provided far more in-depth coverage than did the newspaper or offline editions. The current phase of the network era news presents a complex mingling of future and legacy product. Newspapers have barely changed except to grow thinner. Their once-shadow presences online have grown and come to life. Indeed virtual-world ever-changing websites now cast shadows into the real world that appear as inanimate ink-stained table coverings in cafés. Professional and social news content mingle. Content that makes up the "head" and "tail" have a dialectic relationship, each borrowing from and changing the other.

The 2009 UN Climate Summit brought together politicians, activists, scientists, pop stars, and the public. The object was to reach an agreement to curb carbon emissions by 2015. The summit was covered by independent and commercial news organizations, activist groups and individuals, non-governmental organizations, government and intergovernmental agencies using old and new media tools and practices. The coverage demonstrates the ways the lines that formerly separated the participants, reporters, and audiences have grown dim and elastic and how competition within the expanded journalistic field has receded, changing the products and practices.

Despite innovations taking place in other areas of the newsroom in terms of shifts in practices and products, traditional newspaper coverage within and outside the U.S. followed the predictable patterns and forms of coverage, amplifying bureaucratically credible sources and reflecting national interests. According to content analysis of coverage from national papers in eighteen different countries around the world, the papers domesticated the event frequently by using national political actors as sources for their stories and by focusing coverage on national issues and actors. Forty-two percent of sources used across all of the coverage analyzed were national political actors, clearly demonstrating that the news was largely shaped by political elites and from national perspectives. We can see how editorials published just after the end of the summit typically served to legitimize the actions of domestic politicians. For example, a story from Xinhua news agency published in *China Daily* (December 26, 2009) emphasized Wen Jiabao, Premier of the State Council of China, as a friend of the global South by highlighting his efforts to meet with "island countries and underdeveloped nations for over two hours, the longest during his stay at Copenhagen." Towards the conclusion, the story says, "China showed the greatest sincerity, tried its best and played a constructive part." The *New York Times*, similarly celebrated Barack Obama's role in the otherwise disappointing negotiations: "President Obama deserves much of the credit. He arrived as the talks were collapsing, spent 13 hours in non-stop negotiations and played hardball with the Chinese. With time running out – and with the help of China, India, Brazil and South Africa – he forged an agreement that all but a handful of the 193 nations on hand accepted" (December 21, 2009). German *Bild Zeitung* wrote that "All hopes again are put on Angela Merkel. . . . A lot will be up as to whether she succeeds in taking more care of the interests of the emerging and developing nations. In that case . . . the climate chancellor will become mother earth" (December 20, 2009). South Africa's *Business Day*, meanwhile, praised national leaders for "punching above [their] weight" at COP15 (December 21, 2009) (Kunelisu & Eide 2010). While the traditional press around the world celebrated national political elites, there was a burgeoning field of discourse among the alternative and online journalists that more thoroughly communicated the complexity and diversity of information and opinions related to the summit.

New Partnerships, Platforms, Practices

The summit saw journalists in official and unofficial partnerships with groups that they once reported on – for example, the
Copenhagen News Collaborative set up by politically liberal
investigative magazines *Mother Jones* and *The Nation*, and the
environmental advocacy online outlet TreeHugger – to create
an alternative news wire of about forty reporters, editors, and
commentators. This allowed news outlets lacking equipment and
reporters, especially for international and investigative reporting, to use NGO networks as a resource to spread information
quickly. NGOs, in turn, reaped the benefit of comprehensive and
sympathetic reporting. The participatory media hub and training
center The Uptake, which trains so-called "citizen" journalists to
use innovative methods of low-cost information gathering and
reporting, such as live broadcasting from cell phone camera feeds,
shared resources in Copenhagen with many of the members of
the Copenhagen News Collaborative, including *No Logo* author
Naomi Klein, as well as various NGOs, offering tech support and
reporting resources, and at the same time posting footage and
reports on its own site.

COP15 coverage reflected a more complex model of new media
than had been seen during other recent global protest events,
where citizen media was a crucial source for alternative news
and views on what was happening on the ground. Broken Atlas
blogger Craille Maguire Gillies (2010) describes a media landscape where the divisions between legacy media, social media,
Twitter, traditional reporting, and civic society had dissolved: "It
was citizen journalism at its newest and rawest – a classic example
of a nimble group of camera-wielding documentarians infiltrating
areas traditional media either couldn't access or didn't have the
resources to cover." Activists, advocates, and journalists worked
together to create the raw material – the audio, visual, and textual
products that were then made into stories, reports, and feeds for a
variety of contexts and publics.

These different streams of media were brought together on the
web on platforms like Climate Pulse, created by the Italian online

platform development company eVectors, to demonstrate their new product, which monitors and aggregates blog posts, news websites, Twitter, and a wide range of other sources and adds both a social and editorial layer. The editorial layer allows curators to highlight specific pieces of content. The social layer allows users to tag, rate, comment on, or add various evaluation criteria to each story. For example, users were asked to identify their work-based affiliation – energy business, business, government, environmental NGO, or journalist – and to label pieces of content either a problem or a solution. The data were then aggregated according to tags, so that, for example, if you click on the tag "nuclear energy," a graph appears showing how each of the five categories of users voted. Users can thus easily see what issues people agree and disagree about. Climate Pulse widgets also allow the content to be available on third-party sites, and feedback, ratings, and comments from users of their widgets can feed back into the general flow of Climate Pulse.

Both the Copenhagen News Collaborative and Climate Pulse combine rich media from a variety of genres, including advocacy journalism, analysis, straight reports, dispatches from the scene, background, and so on, from a variety of sources, including professional journalists, activist, NGOs, scientists, politicians, and so on.

Mainstream news outlets also pooled resources and attempted to connect with the public and generate user content. Associated Press (AP) and ten other international news agencies, including France's AFP, Portugal's LUSA, and Russia's RIA Novosti, for example, created Climate Pool, a Facebook page that facilitated communication between the public and journalists covering COP15. In Copenhagen, one of the six AP reporters assigned to cover Copenhagen took the lead each day in interacting with readers. Some traditional newspapers also served as a hub of a diversity of info and media-rich reports on the summit. In tech-savvy news outlets like the *Guardian* and the *New York Times* the use of Twitter and their social networking sites and blogs became an integral part of the coverage.

The *New York Times* blog DotEarth was the hub of the outlet's media-rich and interactive coverage. Andrew Revkin, lead environmental reporter, posted videos, images, podcasts, and text reports from on the ground in Copenhagen, which drew from a diversity of perspectives. His photos were also posted offsite on the photo-sharing site Flickr, a radical departure from the standard practice of the *New York Times* and most commercial news outlets, whose work is protected under strict all rights reserved copyright protection that does not allow it to be shared or reused.

The *New York Times* also hosted a "Climate Change Conversation," where people could post and respond to comments about the climate change debate and on COP15 by clicking on boxes that house the conversations about that topic. The boxes are sized according to the number of comments posted about each topic over the previous forty-eight hours. By the end of 2009 there were 334 comments from twenty-seven different countries. The *New York Times* also supplied readers with background information about the talks in the form of multimedia features such as a timeline of emissions and diplomacy since 1820 and an explainer "Who is at the Climate Talks and what do they seek," which outlines each country's stance and includes maps tagged with emissions, population density, and other data. This combination of sophisticated multimedia and interactive features and its engagement with the larger web and sources normally getting limited exposure, such as protesters, demonstrates that the *New York Times* coverage was far more robust online than offline.

New Relationships between Emergent and Traditional Media

The use of digital tools during the summit moved beyond the pattern of call-and-response relationship with mainstream media that was typical of previous global news events like the 2005 French riots (Russell 2007) and the 2004 Republican National Convention (Gillies 2010). Rather than simply responding to one another, the speed and proliferation and variety of digital tools have heightened the exchange and are further blurring the lines. Several cases illustrated the emergence of a more synergistic relationship between online and offline practices and products.

The double life of reporters

Andrew Revkin is one of the most high-profile and well-respected environmental journalists in the United States. His print stories on COP15 took the traditional form and were framed from the perspectives of the officials who informed the stories. He wrote thirty-six blog posts over the twenty-two-day period of the summit, which used a less formal writing style and were often more in-depth, and appeared alongside a Twitter feed of dynamic info coming in from Copenhagen, and linked out to the wealth of information and opinions available on the web.[2] Revkin walked a sometimes-contentious line between what he referred to as "front page and home page reporting." His first feature-length article on climate change ran in *Discover Magazine* in 1988 and his career has been spent exploring the question of how the world can grow to a projected population of 9 billion people over the next forty years with as little damage as possible (Folkenflick 2009). This question draws vitriol from those who see climate change as a left-wing conspiracy. In October 2009, for example, conservative talk show host Rush Limbaugh suggested Revkin should take his own life to reduce carbon emissions. "If he really thinks that human beings, in their natural existence, are going to cause the extinction of life on Earth," Limbaugh asked, "Mr. Revkin, why don't you just go kill yourself, and help the planet by dying?" Limbaugh and others accuse Revkin of being a part of a radical environmentalist fringe.

Just before the start of COP15, the *New York Times* came under fire for its treatment of coverage of the hacked emails of some prominent climate scientists that it says show a conspiracy among scientists to overstate human influence on the climate. Some accused Revkin of having "a conflict of interest" because he wrote or is mentioned in some of the email messages that the University of East Anglia says were stolen. Others wondered why the *New York Times* did not make the emails available on its website, and scoffed at an explanation by Revkin in a blog post that they contain "private information and statements that were never intended for the public eye." Others accused the *New York Times* of playing down a story with global implications.

After outlining the positions of Revkin's critics and supporters, *New York Times* Ombudsman Clark Hoyt (2009) wrote in his column on the issue:

> I read all the messages involving Revkin, and I did not see anything to keep him off the story. If anything, there was an indication that the scientists whom some readers accused Revkin of being too cozy with were wary of his independence. One, Michael Mann of Pennsylvania State University, warned a colleague, Phil Jones, director of the Climatic Research Unit at East Anglia, to be careful what he shared with "Andy" because, "He's not as predictable as we'd like."

By pointing to Revkin's neutrality and lack of advocacy for climate scientists, Hoyt defends Revkin and the *New York Times* coverage by defending the norms of traditional journalism, claiming he was acting neutrally. Yet the value of Revkin as a journalist is not that he is neutral but that his expertise and skill allow him to convey complicated issues to the public. He is no more neutral about climate change issues than a war reporter is when covering the enemy. Hoyt's defense downplays the value of Revkin's work and at the same time fails to account for why the *New York Times* did not give "equal" space, or practically any space, to the climate skeptics who crowd their comment rooms, the comment sections of other news sites, the blogosphere, and social networking sites. In the new era of journalism, networked publics understand the decision of what to cover and how to cover it, for better or for worse, to be subjective. Beyond balance or objectivity, networked publics expect transparency. Similarly, *The Toronto Star* environmental reporter Tyler Hamilton wrote thirteen stories for his paper between December 1 and 22, and posted twenty-eight times on his blog Clean Break, which includes this disclaimer: "this blog is a personal project started in April 2005. It is not an official blog of the newspaper." Like Revkin, Hamilton's stories follow traditional journalism norms and include standard reports covering environmental policy, energy issues, sustainability, and the emerging clean technology movement. On the blog, Hamilton is much more opinionated. He clearly distinguishes the blogger voice from his institutional voice at the *Star*. Both he and Revkin are operating differently depending on which platform they are writing for. As a blogger there is more space to be critical, more opportunity to provide and link to rich media and contextual information and source material, while within the institutional setting (the *Star* or the *New York Times*) their stories are more constrained by form, space, and tradition.

Fringe points of view making it into the mainstream
Both climate skeptics and summit protesters, two fringe perspectives, were robustly represented in the COP15 coverage, in part because of social media platforms and networks making them more easily accessible and harder to deny. Climate skeptics made their way into the mainstream media often through social media channels. Through comments on major U.S., Canadian, and U.K. media outlets as well as international web platforms like Climate Pool, the voices of climate skeptics at times dominated the discourse, and while they did not overtake the coverage in the official news stories, they did occasionally make their way into mainstream debates. For example, Canadian blogger and climate skeptic Steve McIntyre's posts fact-checking scientific data presented by climate scientists Climate Audit and his highly trafficked blog were sited during COP15 and even won him interviews with the *Wall Street Journal* and CNN. He was able to get his voice into the COP15 coverage without any funding or expertise.

On the opposite side of the political spectrum, new media also gave voice to activists protesting what they saw as flaws in the negotiations and in corporate and governmental climate policy in general. For example, when The Yes Men became part of the COP15 news cycle by announcing in a spoof press release that Canada would make an ambitious 40 percent cut in its emissions by 2020 versus its 1990 levels, and 80 percent by 2050, Climate Pool arranged a real-time web question and answer session with the pranksters. People asked questions via Facebook and Twitter about the group's aims and tactics, deepening the coverage of the spoof and engaging networked publics in story. The group took questions about their motivations, strategies, alliances, and larger goals. For example, someone asked what lessons the group have taken away from their hoaxes. The Yes Men said they felt their message didn't get across as clearly as they'd hoped, explaining they had wanted people to learn "about Canada's true nature and their responsibility to the developing countries" over climate debt. Another question was if the prank undermined the "real debate among real scientists." They replied that there isn't a debate among scientists, there is a consensus, but said they'd hoped the spoof would be "a good distraction to get countries on the right path" and that they were "trying to get something on the table that's the human thing to do – pay debts, reduce emissions." This interactive forum broke the mold of typical protest coverage by providing a platform for The Yes Men to further communicate the issues they were addressing and the critique they were making.

The *New York Times* uncharacteristically framed protesters in a positive light. It ran a handful of stories which focused on protesters and members of NGOs and other civic groups, emphasizing both their legitimate criticism of the summit and their civil behavior. For example, one *New York Times* story describes some of the groups outside the Bella Center:

> The thousands of non-governmental organizations, which are normally central to international climate conferences, found themselves locked out. . . . The environmental groups here played the roles of both advocate and expert, given that they follow the focal issues year after year. They are observers – and entertainers, organizing colorful and startling protests. And they provide logistical support and translation for people in some of the poorest countries, who often lack the resources to relay their message on their own. (December 19, 2009)

Unlike typical news coverage of activists that treats them as forces of violence and conflict (Atton & Hamilton 2008; Gitlin 1980; Kellner 1992), this more sympathetic coverage of those outside the political elite suggests that the journalism field is expanding not only online but also within the traditional outlets and among professional journalists.

Discussion: Beyond Storytelling – The Changing Role of Journalists

Illustration of the networked news environment through COP15 coverage demonstrates the dramatic way the field of journalism is expanding through new partnerships, platforms, and practices. Journalists are joining forces with each other and with networked publics; they are taking a stance that climate change is a real and important issue; and they are doing their work differently and creating new forms and styles of news for the pages of the newspaper and the pages of the web. Online the coverage unfolded in real time with rich media content and interactive platforms deepening the information coming from Copenhagen and the dialogue it spurred. Publics interested in in-depth coverage had an extraordinary range of choices to consume, comment on, recommend, aggregate, contribute to, and engage with in order to connect with what was going on in Copenhagen. While one of the major functions of the news media was to hold officials at the negotiating table accountable, new- and old-style journalists clearly found dynamic ways to facilitate deliberation and to include a plurality of voices and perspectives in the coverage – for example, by eliciting conversations with the public through collaborative efforts like the Facebook page Climate Pool, where a collective of international news agencies reached out to the public; platforms like Climate Pulse that allowed people to contribute to and curate the diversity of material hosted there; and in spaces like the *New York Times* "Climate Change Conversation" – in the process creating a more pluralistic field of news around COP15.

COP15 coverage showed that journalism is no longer exclusively about storytelling or even about producing a final product. New forms of journalism emerging include platforms that enable communities to share what they know and need to know; algorithms that aggregate and cluster and prioritize news; and collaboration and crowdsourcing which feed into the process of circulation of information and do not always end up in story form. News about COP15 came in the forms of Twitter streams, in a snapshot of current knowledge (see, for example, the Wikipedia page on the 2010 United Nations Climate Change Conference). And these new forms demand that journalists master new skills and expand their professional identities. Journalists today need to be community organizers, teachers, curators, filters, tool-makers, and collaborators.

COP15 coverage also demonstrates that networked journalism is about sustaining and shaping a continual work in progress, identifying ever-multiplying information resources and helping shape the information environment, rather than creating a final product. Beat and daily reporters in the networked era keep pace with the participatory 24/7 experience of news publics. Instead of trying to produce a perfect "final" product daily, weekly, or monthly, journalists working online must produce new content on a near-constant cycle. This shift from the mentality of a "final product" to a "work in progress" (or several smaller works over the course of a day) also means anticipating and embracing the fact that the content will be immediately commented upon, repurposed, or enhanced by users.

Aggregation is part of this "reporting" process. So-called "findability" has become paramount in an environment where the first line of user participation is choosing what content to access. Because of this, sites like Climate Pulse became the center of a vibrant community of people seeking real-time information and responses to COP15 and larger issues related to the climate crisis drawn from diverse streams of information. News publics not only filter and curate, they mash up personal news and news of current events and issue news of widespread interest. People have integrated journalism into their personal communities, sharing news items, adding their opinions. According to Nick Bilton, lead technology writer/reporter for the *New York Times'* "Bits Blog" and former researcher in the paper's Research & Development Labs:

> The relevance of news is changing. When Teddy Kennedy died that wasn't news to me but it was to a lot of people. There was a shooting across the street from my house: that was news to me, but not to you, unless you live where I live. Our concepts of news are changing. If someone in my friend's network gets in a car accident that's news to me. (Barenblat 2009)

During COP15 we could see the integration of personal and professional networks on Twitter feeds of activists and journalists alike who peppered dispatches about the negotiations and the scene on the ground in Copenhagen with personal observations, experiences, and news.

The importance of building meaningful networked communities demands that journalists interact with users who are not professionally trained as journalists, sharing resources, engaging them in conversation, "crowdsourcing" investigations, fact-checking, story recommending, and more. This was clearly going on in the coverage of COP15, for example, when activist group Uptake shared resources with the Copenhagen News Collaborative, when journalists collectively engaged the Facebook publics with Climate Pool, and in the pages of comment and discussion on the *New York Times* "Climate Change Conversation." Collaboration among journalists both within the same news organizations and among competing organizations is also a key feature of this new environment. Despite a legacy of competition, journalists inside and outside mainstream news organizations are sharing resources and linking to one another's work. Andrew Revkin and other key climate journalists linked out to content on the web and embedded Twitter feeds on their blogs. Increasingly news is being designed to be shared: for example, Propublica creates stories and content to give away free to any news organization that will run them. APIs developed by the *New York Times* and other news organizations allow people to mash up news content. The site Reportingon allows reporters to share Twitter-like updates on stories they are covering. Today, more important for a journalist than being first on a story is bringing his or her readers the best journalistic efforts on a particular topic, even when those efforts have appeared in other publications.

The increased and widespread importance of collaboration also influences the habits of news publics. Online communication and social networking platforms have reached a scale where mass conversation and "social reading" is becoming a central metaphor for new media. As the Pew numbers show, news is now "a shared social experience as people swap links in emails, post news stories on their social networking site feeds, highlight news stories in their tweets, and debate the meaning of events in discussion threads" (Purcell et al. 2010). In effect, the solitary act of news reading or watching is ending, which in turn changes the act of writing and reporting news. "Since reading and watching television was an individual act, the journalists' role as an educator was paramount. People learned about current affairs privately, which equip them to interact publicly. With social reading, people learn about current affairs and engage with others at the same time. Journalists become conveners, facilitators and instigators in an inquiry process . . ." (Deifell 2009: 17).

According to Pew, 72 percent of Americans who follow the news say they talk with friends, family, and colleagues about what is happening in the world. Further, it's not just that people are discussing; many of us are beginning to include news organizations, journalists, and other media personalities in our social networks. People, for example, are "friending" journalists on Facebook and following them on Twitter (Purcell et al. 2010).

In light of the shift from personalization to socialization, the increased collaboration among journalists and between journalists and networked publics, and the increasingly engaged habits of news publics, as reflected by the Pew numbers, the idea of the long tail needs revision. It is clearly no longer exclusively a business concept; rather it is a way of looking at the dynamic between mainstream and niche content and how people navigate and organize it for themselves or through news organizations that are at the forefront of creating this new architecture. COP15 coverage demonstrates that when niche and mainstream news exist, the tail and the head are connected in a continuum, the two influencing one another. It no longer makes sense to see the two as separate. The availability of marginal, niche, and non-market journalism products is influencing what news producers and publics know as well as how they engage with the news.

These shifts signal new opportunities for public engagement and an emphasis on facilitating discourse from a diversity of sources, creating more plurality in the news landscape. Involving the public has become an economic imperative for the news industry, and public involvement – everything from reporting the news to simply posting a link on Facebook – has become part of the relationship between news and networked publics. Networked publics are replacing passive consumers and, together with digital tools and news industry economics, changing the way journalism is produced, circulated, and discussed.

Notes

1 In 2003 *New York Times* journalist Jayson Blair was fired for plagiarism and for the fabrication of interviews and other source material for stories he wrote for the paper.

2 During COP15, Twitter became a dynamic way to follow and contribute to reports and discussion of what was happening in Copenhagen. This in fact became standard practice among journalists to follow breaking news and commentary and to post and publicize their own work and commentary. Along with "Santa Claus" and "Tiger Woods," "Copenhagen" became during the summit a "trending topic" on Twitter, a gauge of popularity based on the frequency of the posts including the term.

References

Allan, S. (2006) *Online News*. Maidenhead: Open University Press.

Anderson, C. (2006) *The Long Tail: Why the Future of Business is Selling Less of More*. New York: Hyperion.

API Documentation and Tools (2010) http://developer.nytimes.com/docs/campaign_finance_api

Atton, C. & Hamilton, J.F. (2008) *Alternative Journalism*. New York: Sage.

Aufderheide, P., Clark, J., Nisbet, M.C., Dessauer, C., & Donnell, K. (2009) "Scan and Analysis of Best Practices in Digital Journalism in and outside U.S. Public Broadcasting." Center for Social Media Report. http://www.centerforsocialmedia.org/future-public-media/documents/white-papers/scan-and-analysis-best-practices-digital-journalism-and-o

Barenblat, R. (2009) "Nick Bilton on Multitasking and Media." Poptech, October 24. http://www.poptech.org/blog/nick_bilton_on_multitasking_and_media

Benkler, Y. (2006) *The Wealth of Networks: How Social Production Transforms Markets and Freedom*. New Haven: Yale University Press.

Blood, R. (2000) "Weblogs: A History and Perspective." Rebecca's Pocket, September 7. http://www.rebeccablood.net/essays/weblog_history.html

Boyd, D. & Ellison, N. (2007) "Social Network Sites: Definition, History, and Scholarship." *Journal of Computer-Mediated Communication* 13:1. http://jcmc.indiana.edu/vol13/issue1/boyd.ellison.html

Bruns, A. (2005) *Gatewatching: Collaborative Online News Production*. New York: Peter Lang.

Carey, J. (1998) "Communication, Culture and Technology: An Interview with James W. Carey." *Journal of Communication Inquiry* 22:2, 117–30.

Deifell, T. (2009) "The Big Thaw: Charting the New Future of Journalism." The Media Consortium. http://www.themediaconsortium.org/thebigthaw/

Emmett, A. (2009) "Networking News." *American Journalism Review*, December/January. http://www.ajr.org/article.asp?id=4646

Folkenflick, D (2009). "Innovative 'Times' Reporter Draws Limbaugh's Ire." NPR.org, October 22. http://www.npr.org/templates/story/story.php?storyId=114029917

Gillies, C.M. (2010) "Activist Journalists Bring Citizen and Professional Media Together." Broken Atlas. http://www.brokenatlas.com/2010/01/19/activist-journalists-bring-citizen-pro-media-together-at-cop15/

Gillmor, D. (2004) *We the Media*. Cambridge, MA: O'Reilly Media.

Gitlin, T. (1980) *The Whole World is Watching*. Berkeley: University of California Press.

Holovaty, A (2006) "A Fundamental Way Newspaper Sites Need to Change." Holovaty.com. http://www.holovaty.com/writing/fundamental-change/

Hoyt, C (2009) "Stolen E-Mail, Stoking the Climate Debate." *New York Times*, December 6. http://www.nytimes.com/2009/12/06/opinion/06pubed.html?_r=3&ref=opinion

Kellner, D. (1992) The Persian Gulf TV War. Boulder, CO:Westview Press.

Kunelius, R. & Eide, E. (eds) (2010) *Reading the Environment: An International Analysis of Press Discourses on the Climate Crisis*. Gothenburg: Nordicom.

Lasica, J.D (2002) "The Promise of the Daily Me." Online Journalism Review, April 2. http://www.ojr.org/ojr/lasica/1017779142.php

Lenhart, A., Purcell, K., Smith, A., & Zickuhr, K. (2010) "Social Media and Young Adults." Pew Internet and American Life Project, February. http://www.pewinternet.org/Reports/2010/Social-Media-and-Young-Adults.aspx

Lowrey, W (2006) "Mapping the Journalism–Blogging Relationship." *Journalism* 7:4, 477–500.

Meyer, K. (2006) "The Best of the Worst." *The Wall Street Journal*, May 3. http://online.wsj.com/article/SB114424637699117715.html

Negroponte, N. (1995) *Being Digital*. Cambridge, MA: MIT Press.

O'Reilly, T. (2005) "What is Web 2.0?" O'Reilly, September 30. http://oreilly.com/web2/archive/what-is-web-20.html?page=1

Purcell, K, Rainie, L., Mitchell, A., Rosenstiel, T., & Olmstead, K. (2010) "Understanding the Participatory News Consumer." Pew Internet and American Life Project, March 1. http://www.pewinternet.org/Reports/2010/Online-News.aspx

Rainie, L. (2005) "The State of Blogging." Pew Internet and American Life Project, January 2. http://www.pewinternet.org/Reports/2005/The-State-of-Blogging.aspx

Rainie, L. & Anderson, J. (2008) "The Future of the Internet III." Pew Internet and American Life Project, December 14. http://www.pewinternet.org/Reports/2008/The-Future-of-the-Internet-III.aspx

Robinson, S. (2006) "The Mission of the j-Blog: Recapturing Journalistic Authority Online." *Journalism* 7, 64.

Russell, A. (2007) "Digital Communication Networks and the Journalistic Field," *Critical Studies in Media Communication* 24:4, 285–302.

Singer, J. (2001) "The Metro Wide Web: Changes in Newspapers' Gatekeeping Role Online." *Journalism and Mass Communication Quarterly* 78:1, 39–56.

Sunstein, C. (2002) *Republic.com*. Princeton, N.J.: Princeton University Press.

Titus, R. (2007) "A Lick of Paint for the BBC Homepage." BBC, December 13. http://www.bbc.co.uk/blogs/bbcinternet/2007/12/a_lick_of_paint_for_the_bbc_ho.html

Wellman, B. (1988) "Structural Analysis: From Method and Metaphor to Theory and Substance." In: B. Wellman & S.D. Berkowitz (eds), *Social Structures: A Network Approach*. Cambridge, UK: Cambridge University Press.

World Association of Newspapers (2007) "How Young People Use Media: Youth DNA Study Measures Trends." http://www.wan-press.org/article14281.html

4

News Parody, Satire, Remix

When There's Nothing to Do but Laugh

["Fake news"] can hardly be charged with being illegitimate journal-ism.

Geoffrey Baym (2005)

In what Gawker (2009b) described as "possibly the most painfully funny Daily Show skit ever produced," Jason Jones visited the *New York Times* building in June 2009 and ridiculed both staff and product in *The Daily Show*'s trademark style of mock serious-ness and professionalism. In the skit Jones relentlessly hammers on network-era weaknesses of the *New York Times*, painting the paper as a relic of a bygone era. "Whether it's uncovering what's happening during a war, leading us into that war in the first place or just making shit up, the *Times* covers the news like no one else."

On the most superficial level, the skit comments on the receding power of what Jones calls "aged" news, and exploits the ideologi-cal and economic struggles taking place between traditional and emerging journalism and news industry business models. Jones, however, is also offering another dimension to his critique: he remixes and re-appropriates "news" by playing the role of the journalist, asking pointed questions, and treating his "sources" for the piece, the editors at the *New York Times*, to a satirically familiar air of moral and professional authority. It's an old trick, a brand of social critique used in particular against authority for at least the past four decades. Jones was borrowing, knowingly or not, from the French Situationists by, in the words of Guy Debord, "developing a counter discourse through stealing, plagiarizing, and expropriating speech, through reversing dominant meanings and accepted usages" (McDonough 2007: 5).

In response to the rise of "fake" news shows like Comedy Central's *The Daily Show* and to the anxiety that the popularity of such shows has generated (Kalin 2006), many studies have theorized the social and political value of these programs as tools of resistance (Baym 2004; Boler & Turpin 2008; Gray et al. 2009; Jones 2004). Media scholar Geoffrey Baym argues, for example, that satire and parody are effective tools in interrogating power and deconstructing news. More generally he says,

> Comedy . . . provides the ethos to engage in serious political criticism; the label of "fake news" enables *The Daily Show* to say that which the traditional journalist can not. So too does its categorization as comedy grant it immunity from accusations that it violates journalistic standards. Never claiming to be news, it can hardly be charged with being illegitimate journalism; either by the political structure it interrogates or the news media it threatens. (2004: 20)

Others have demonstrated the quality of content and the knowledge and sophistication of audiences. Jones, in a study comparing the content of *The Daily Show* and CNN, concludes that "The public is well aware that both television and politics are spectacle performances and, indeed, that the press and government are two mutually reinforcing and constituting institutions. . . . An increasingly media-savvy public realizes that news programs such as CNN are no more "real" than *The Daily Show* is "fake"' (2004: 20). Jonathan Gray, Jeffrey Jones, and Ethan Thompson in their book *Satire TV: Politics and Comedy in the Post-Network Era* argue that while traditional news forms posit politics as something to learn, satire challenges news publics to examine, question, and play with politics rather than simply to consume it (2009: 11).

"Fake" news is a flourishing form of networked public culture in large part due to the dramatic changes in how television has conducted business over the past two decades. The rise of cable narrowcasting has allowed for popular political critique in the form of fake news to flourish, but it cannot account for its resonance with audiences (Gray et al. 2009). The wild success of shows like Jon Stewart's *The Daily Show*, among others, suggests that fake news is both a product of and an antidote to the particular challenges faced by contemporary global culture. It draws on corporate news media culture, mocks it, offers people an alternative, and contributes to the construction of forms of engagement that are acting partly at least to revive civic culture in the form of what cultural scholars Megan Boler and Steven Turpin (2008) have termed "ironic citizenship." Contrary to the assertions of those who claim fake news signals cynicism and a breakdown of civic engagement, by employing the ethos and aesthetic of remix, fake news is contributing to the blurring of the lines among genres and styles and in doing so re-appropriating mainstream news materials, formats, and personalities in order to challenge particular notions of truth and journalism.

Situating the phenomenon of fake news historically by examining its connections to détournement and the Situationist International movement, and within more recent practices of remix and appropriation, this chapter highlights the context in which these modes of resistance first developed and discusses the ways in which they have shifted owing to the specific conditions of the networked media environment. The chapter then examines the content, coverage, and online response to two different cases where fake news became part of the mainstream media landscape: Colbert's guest-edited issue of *Newsweek*; and The Yes Men's fake editions of the *New York Times* and *New York Post*. By focusing on examples of how fake news is both being adopted by mainstream professional journalists and outlets, and being taken up and infused into the news landscape by activists, influencing the news agenda and expanding the discourse, the chapter highlights the complex ways "fake" news is influencing the journalism landscape not only in terms of how people relate to the news but also in the process of news creation. Drawing from these examples and other studies that address news parody and satire as political forms, the chapter suggests ways that parody, remix, and appropriation are influencing both notions of citizenship and of journalism, and facilitating new forms of political engagement.

Détournement in Context

Modernization and the introduction of consumer society after World War II inspired the Situationist International (SI), a small group of French cultural and political revolutionaries in the 1950s and 1960s, to build a movement around their critique of mass media and advertising that attempted to undermine what they saw as capitalism's totalitarian influence. In *The Society of the Spectacle* Guy Debord argues that under capitalism life is reduced to an immense accumulation of mere appearances where "all that once was directly lived has become mere representation" (1967: thesis 1). The spectacle he writes, "presents itself as something enormously positive, indisputable and inaccessible. It says nothing more than 'that which appears is good, that which is good appears.' The attitude which it demands in principle is passive acceptance which in fact is already obtained by its manner of appearing without reply, by its monopoly of appearance." Ultimately the spectacle is "the moment when the commodity has attained the total occupation of the social life" (2001: thesis 42). The media in essence are the spectacle, with films and advertising, for example, providing a collage of music, images, and narratives that promotes the irresistible benefits and attraction of contemporary life and the technical and institutional apparatus that drives it.

To undermine the spectacle, the Situationists used détournement, or what they described as "the excision of an item of culture (whether image, text, or object) from its normative context and its subsequent juxtaposition with another fragment in order to establish an analogical relationship between the two" (McDonough 2007: 5). That is, in order to resist the spectacle, the Situationists advocated remixing the raw material from which it was built in order to parody or satirize its original meaning or form.

Remix: Contemporary Détournement

Détournement is the historical precursor to remix, the practice which is accelerated in the contemporary media environment by digital technology that allows people to easily obtain the tools and skills to create expressive work that includes elements of a previously created work. Sampling in music making is a prime example, whereby musicians take a portion of one sound recording and use it as an instrument in the creation of another recording or a song. This practice is also being employed when fans recast narratives in videos starring characters from their favorite shows, activists remix political speeches and commercials on video to create new-style political and social commentary, cultural critics recast advertisements to subvert their message, and bloggers comb over the facts presented in mainstream news reports. Some argue that this practice of re-appropriation through remix has become the fundamental logic of cultural consumption (Jenkins 2005; Lessig 2008; Manovich 2001). In the words of remix musician and author Paul Miller aka DJ Spooky, remix is "play and irreverence towards the found objects that we use as consumers and a sense that something new was right in front of our oh so jaded eyes" (2004: 45).

In this environment where the public takes a more active role – where everyone is a potential journalist and where meta-news and coverage of the coverage disrupt the spectacle of the news – a more critical eye has been cast toward professional news. In September 2009 Pew reported that the public's assessment of the accuracy of news stories was at its lowest level in more than two decades. Their survey data showed that 29 percent of Americans say that news organizations generally get the facts straight, while 63 percent say that news stories are often inaccurate. The same survey in 1985 found 55 percent believed news stories were accurate while 34 percent said they were inaccurate. That percentage had fallen sharply by the late 1990s and has remained low over the last decade. Sixty percent of the 2009 respondents say news organizations are politically biased (Pew 2009).

In journalism, as with most cultural industries, the aesthetics and practice of remix are synergistic: for example, both traditional and new-style journalists create news-related content on blogs, Twitter, and other social networking sites – poaching the styles and news-related content from one another. And while mainstream news is tapping into new forms and practices of journalism to remain relevant and repair the legitimacy crisis they currently face, Henry Jenkins (2005) suggests that the new environment offers fresh opportunities for mainstream and resistant media to share the media landscape and engage in a dialogic rather than disruptive exchange. He argues that a shift has occurred in the nature of resistance from culture jamming to what he describes as poaching and what I call remixing. To him jamming refers to "efforts to introduce noise into the signal as it passes from transmitter to receiver and assumes that the masses are vulnerable to manipulation" (2005: 214). Culture jammers want to disrupt media power while remixers what to share it. Fans, for example, see unrealized potential in popular culture and want to broaden audience participation. Jenkins writes,

> Fan culture is dialogic rather than disruptive, affective more than ideological, and collaborative rather than confrontational. Similarly, bloggers take knowledge in their own hands, enabling successful navigation within and between these emerging knowledge cultures. One can see such behavior as cooptation into commodity culture in so far as it sometimes collaborates with corporate interests, but one can also see it increasing the diversity of media culture, providing opportunities for greater inclusiveness, and making commodity culture more responsive to consumers (2002:168).

Remix, while it can be used as a method of culture jamming, in its most potent execution borrows from old forms to re-create, rather than jam or stop, the original product.

Fake News as Remix

Fake news programs employ a form of remix – they employ parody, irony, and/or satire to imitate popular news forms, sources, and content in order to critique them. They are thus fake not so much because they are less than authentic but because they expose the "fakeness" of the so-called "real" news. Shows like *The Daily Show* do this by blurring lines between the genres of comedy, entertainment talk shows, and news to an extent that has never before taken place and in doing so create a sort of remix of the discourse that takes place within these genres. The blurring of these boundaries suggests an increased recognition that they are in place to serve the interests of the powerful industries and political entities as well as an increased willingness to challenge the structures of political and social power (Delli Carpini & Williams 2001; Druick 2009). According to Baym, this discursive integration is a way of understanding and expressing the world, which is now defined by "the permeability of form and fluidity of content." He writes:

> Discourses of news, politics, entertainment and marketing have grown deeply inseparable; the language, styles, and practices of each have lost their distinctiveness and are being remolded and melded into previously unthought combinations. For some this is a narrative of crisis, but the contemporary media environment also contains the potential for a worthwhile rethinking of discursive styles and standards that occasionally opens spaces for significant innovation. (2004: 6)

Just as Walter Benjamin (2001) argued that mass-produced and mass-circulated images would have a profound democratic impact by, among other things, eroding the "aura" surrounding works of high art and dethroning cultural authorities and inspiring new forms of expertise (such as that of sports fans or movie buffs), blurring the line between popular culture and politics may teach citizens new ways of engagement (Jenkins 2005: 224).

Fake news as both a means to critique news and a way to make it more appealing is nothing new. In 1835, for example, the *New York Sun* ran what came to be known as "The Great Moon Hoax": a series of articles published under the name of a contemporary astronomer described in great detail the discovery of life on the moon. The hoax succeeded in increasing the paper's circulation and creating critical commentary on popular scholarly and religious discourse about outer space, including the claims of Reverend Thomas Dick, wildly popular in the U.S. at the time, to have computed the existence of over 21 million inhabitants in the solar system (Goodman 2008). Famous novelist Samuel Clemens (aka Mark Twain) began his writing career as a newspaper reporter infamous for publishing satirical fiction and passing it off as non-fiction. Clemens explained his hoaxes on the growing hype around the alleged petrification of human bodies – a condition that killed people but then allowed their bodies to remain intact:

> In the fall of 1862, in Nevada, and California, the people got to running wild about extraordinary petrification and other natural marvels. One could scarcely pick up a paper without finding in it one or two glorified discoveries of this kind. The mania was becoming a little ridiculous. . . . I chose to kill the petrification mania with a delicate, very delicate satire. (Clemens as quoted in Tribble 2008: 56–7)

While these hoaxes were using fiction as a means to shed a critical light on false information being passed off as fact, journalists frequently use irony as a device to bring to light corruption and to critique abuses of power perpetrated by those meant to be working in the public interest.

Journalism scholars Ted Glasser and James Ettema explore the frequent use of what they describe as "morally earnest" irony in investigative journalism and what they call the "irony of irony," or the phenomenon whereby "The language intended to advance the discussions about what is true and good may become means to undo those discussions (1998: 89). To them irony transforms objectivity into morally charged vocabulary that can be used to condemn the powers that be. Irony and objectivity don't merely co-exist;" they write, "irony exploits objectivity to work its effect" (1998: 89). Irony out in the world – things like philandering politicians campaigning on a platform of family values – is like a red flag leading investigative journalists to damning facts. Journalistic irony as a force for civic reform, however, does not necessarily spur hope. As Jean Baudrillard put it, "hyperinformation" has dampened the will for collective action and instead moves people to "take their revenge by allowing themselves the theatrical representations of the political scene" (quoted in Glasser & Ettema 1998: 106). And in the same vein philosopher Richard Rorty worried that the ironies of victimization and villainy could be reinterpreted or reinscribed to transform them from moral outrages to cynical jokes, echoing the concerns of those who see the rise of fake news as a sign of increased cynicism (Glasser & Ettema 1998: 106).

Satirical news in the contemporary political, economic, and cultural climate, however, is spurring new forms of media ironies, which are opening new avenues for the circulation of issues and new styles of presenting the news. Croatia's satirical newspaper the *Feral Tribune*, for example, became the only reliable news source in the early 1990s during the war when the country was under threat of occupation and political corruption. It used satire to comment on government corruption and war crimes perpetrated by Croatian soldiers among other topics that were ignored by other national news media. One particularly controversial issue featured a cover with an image of Franjo Tuđman, the Croatian President, and Slobodan Milošević, the Yugoslav President, later convicted by the UN's International Criminal Tribunal for the Former Yugoslavia for crimes against humanity, in bed together – a symbolic condemnation of policies leading to the division of Bosnia-Herzegovina. The *Feral Tribune* continued to publish despite government attempts to put it out of business through lawsuits and new taxes imposed on the paper that normally applied only to publishers of pornographic content, and at least one anonymous death threat against editor Drago Hedl. Ultimately the paper shut down when the government froze its bank account because of unpaid taxes. Despite the fact that its content was satirical and therefore it did not fit neatly into the genre of journalism, the *Feral Tribune* won several prestigious news awards, including in 1996 the International Press Directory's award for freedom of the press; and in 1997 the World Association of Newspaper's Golden Pen of Freedom and an International Press Freedom Award from the Committee to Protect Journalists. Most recently, in 2005, editor Drago Hedl was awarded the Knight International Award for Excellence in Journalism (Boljanovic 2007; *Feral Tribune* 2007). In the context of overt political turmoil and suppression of information, it is clear to the international journalism community and free press advocates that the information provided by *Feral Tribune* journalists was no less news because it came in the form of satire.

Scholars Megan Boler and Steve Turpin, whose work addresses the political and cultural significance of "fake" news, argue that satire is a way of coping with complacency in contemporary society and that it creates what they call "ironic citizenship," a space in which people are invited to participate in public life that acknowledges the spectacle. In their study of responses to Jon Stewart's appearance on *Crossfire*, an infamously combative current events debate show aired by CNN in the U.S., in which he pleaded with the hosts to "stop hurting America" with partisan hackery, they identify the popularity of the event in the perception of Stewart's courage to speak the truth and to confront the role of the media in the ailing political environment in the U.S. They argue that the *Crossfire* episode illustrates "a sincere demand for truthfulness and accountability against a culturally understood backdrop of the . . . spectacular society in which we recognize our complicity" (2008: 395). Networked culture and practices of resistance, to them, represent the plurality of innovative ways in which we overcome complacency in spectacular society:

> Because we tend to recognize, experientially and thus intuitively, the immense planetary problems created through structures of global capitalism and its attendant state institutions (not to mention the media itself), our reality is inevitably one of complacency. However, this complicity, when accompanied by an ironic approach to truth and politics, engenders a correlative critique of spectacular relations. And offers a potential for thinking about new possible relations within the social and political registers. (2008: 387)

The idea that the desire to recuperate our complacency is a common element of contemporary realities is supported by recent studies that demonstrate that audience numbers for fake news shows are on the rise (Pew 2009) and that these audiences are more likely to know the issue positions and backgrounds of presidential candidates than people who do not watch late-night comedy (Jones 2007). They are also more likely to record and share clips of their favorite shows, adopting them to their own purposes, and using them to inform on multiple issues of concern. Boler (2007) writes:

We have discovered that web-based communities sparked by political commentary like *The Daily Show* are vibrant and translating into action. This past week, I interviewed an established blogger who began streaming TDS clips when his Macintosh wouldn't interface with the Comedy Central site, and decided it would be a service to other Mac users to post clips in Quicktime format. As a result, he unexpectedly began to get voluminous traffic from readers around the globe. I asked him if he thought that his site resulted in any action. It was a surprise to me to hear him report that in fact, as he learns from the ongoing conversations and comments posted on his website, that because of viewing and discussing *The Daily Show* many members of this progressive community have been led to activism. Another blogger was inspired to go join Cindy Sheehan's protest in Crawford because of the conversations engaged through his Daily Show postings.

The existence and popularity of comic news do not suggest complacency and apathy but rather a way to engage with the news and public life through a critique of its structures. In the corporate media landscape, which privileges ratings and profits over the public good, comedians like Stewart do what journalists cannot. They abandon neutrality and offer critiques of the social, political, and economic stories, actors, and institution on which they report. And because of the fair-use shield of parody, these fake journalists can, without threat of legal repercussions, report on politicians' lies and corruption, and critique the news media's failures to hold politicians accountable.

In an often-cited exchange between Stewart and Bill Moyers, Moyers (2007) said: "I don't know whether you are practicing an old form of parody and satire . . . or a new form of journalism." Stewart replied: "Well then that either speaks to the sad state of comedy or of the sad state of news. I can't figure out which one. I think, honestly, we're practicing a new form of desperation." This new form of desperation is being manifest around the world as fake news, and it is proving wildly popular with fans not only watching and reading but also recirculating the content. The fake-news genre, of which Stewart is currently the king, is indeed détournement – an old form of parody and satire, and also a new form of journalism, born out of the specific networked conditions, which at once overlaps with traditional news media, at times influencing its agenda and content, and acts as a challenge to it.

Fake News from the Inside

The rise in popularity of comedy news shows has prompted U.S. mainstream journalists and commercial news outlets to adopt news parody and satire, hoping to benefit from its popularity. ABC's *This Week with George Stephanopoulos*, for example, includes a "Funnies" segment, a "best of" roundup of late-night comics, which literally rips and remixes content from other shows, albeit legally. This segment of the show is presumably meant to demonstrate that Stephanopoulos is relevant enough to be in on the joke and in the process it affirms the cultural cachet of political comedy (Achter 2009). In February 2007 Fox debuted the comedy show *½ Hour News Hour*, which delivered fake news from a conservative perspective in the style made famous by *Saturday Night Live Weekend Update* and *The Daily Show*. And CNN Headline News debuted its show *Not Just Another Cable News Show* in April 2008, which featured comedians' perspectives on historical events. Both shows were canceled within a year. This surely came as no surprise to Stephen Colbert, who, in response to a question about the possible success of *½ Hour News Hour* during an appearance at Harvard, gave an uncharacteristically straight response:

> I think conservativism tends to be less iconoclastic and comedy often deals with status shifts. If I want to bore the hell out of you I could talk about status shifts and how you can find one in any joke or any bit of comedy if you wanted to look for it. Going after the status quo is not necessarily a conservative thing to do; its antithetical to the idea of conversativism. Comedy is all about change. So it's going to be a challenge for them. But you know if they are funny I'd only really respect that because it's hard to produce comedy and I'd like something else to watch and to rip off. (Colbert 2006)

While CNN is not considered politically conservative, Colbert's theory of status shifts may also account for the cancelation of the program *Not Just Another Cable News Show* and the lack of attention paid to the "Funnies." Political satire on mainstream news channels must strike a delicate, maybe impossible, balance in challenging the status quo without truly calling the powers that be into question. Colbert came up against this very predicament when he agreed to guest edit an issue of *Newsweek* magazine.

Stephen Colbert as *Newsweek* Guest Editor

For the June 8, 2009 issue of *Newsweek* magazine, Colbert was brought in as first-ever guest editor, which corresponded to his trip to Baghdad, where he taped a week's worth of episodes of his comedy central show *The Colbert Report*, a satirical news show in which he portrays a caricatured version of Tim O'Reilly, the conservative political talk show host. Colbert is the ultimate remix artist – he seamlessly reinvents the conservative talk show host in a way that makes both conservatives and progressives laugh. While the topic of his show is overtly political, he insists he is not in the business of news, and that he merely uses news as material for his comedy. And while his comedy centers on mocking the hubris and "truthiness," or unfounded beliefs, of the conservative right, Colbert fans come from both the political right and left. A recent study "The Irony of Satire" demonstrated that many conservative Colbert fans do not perceive his maniacal, right-wing caricature to be an actual character that he is playing. That is, while people of all creeds find him funny, the authors of the study report that many believe "Colbert only pretends to be joking and genuinely means what he said" (LaMarre et al. 2009: 212).

Colbert's widespread party-crossing appeal most likely helped get him the invitation to edit *Newsweek*. Two weeks earlier *Newsweek* unveiled its new design, which they described as "less daunting, more entertaining and easier to navigate." They announced a new editorial strategy aimed at being "provocative, but not partisan," and a business model "focused on a smaller, more devoted, slightly more affluent audience" (Deveny 2009). Editor Jon Meacham saw Colbert as both a way to cater to the desired demographic and as a way to reengage readers with the Iraq War, which at the time had receded from headlines. Meacham told the *New York Observer* he was impressed with Colbert's "almost encyclopedic feel for anything that came up" (Koblin 2009).

Colbert explains his role in creating the special issue on the Iraq War in an editor's note entitled "Why I Took This Crummy Job": "I took advantage of my powerful new perch and published all my letters to the editor that *Newsweek* had rejected, provided my Conventional Wisdom, took a red pencil to Meacham's editorial foofaraw and took the bias out of the columnist bios. Most important, I sent *Newsweek*'s reporters to find out whatever happened to Iraq."

And in a "Reader's guide" to the issue, editor Jon Meacham explained that Colbert designed the cover, inserted his voice throughout the issue, and selected the features from a set of options presented to him, reassuring readers that "Everything he did in character is signed, so there should be no confusion about what is *Newsweek* and what is Colbert" (Meacham 2009).

Meacham preemptively addressed criticism:

> Some readers and critics will inevitably object, saying that this is a publicity stunt. To them I solemnly say: you are half-right. Of course I am seeking publicity for the magazine. I would argue with the term "stunt," though, but only because of the popular assumption that a stunt is something silly. (The dictionary definition is a feat of daring, but we do not live in the dictionary.) Colbert's involvement is an exercise not in silliness but in satire, and the two are very different things. His role means more attention for *Newsweek*, yes, and to me that is a good thing. It also brings more readers to a serious subject – and that heightened interest is a good thing, too. The test of whether the Colbert decision was a sound one, I think, is whether readers learn something new from the following pages.

In an introduction to a series of features on Iraq, Colbert becomes serious and writes: "My character and I both think it's a shame that we're not talking about the troops anymore." And in the editor's letter he explains that the special edition of *Newsweek* is meant to bring attention to people "who've been touched by [the war], from the citizens in Iraq to the cadets at West Point."

The *Newsweek* issue edited by Colbert generated a great deal of commentary about its content and about *Newsweek* more generally, which demonstrates some anxiety about the blurring of the genres of journalism and comedy as well as a widespread misunderstanding of satire among both media and general audiences.

As Jon Meacham anticipated, the news of Colbert's guest editor role was met with accusations that the move was a marketing ploy. A *Chicago Tribune* commentator wrote: "Instead of admitting it's a naked publicity ploy for the magazine, recently redesigned as a journal of analysis, editor Jon Meacham opted for truthiness, a Colbert coinage" (Johnson 2009). Gawker (2009a) wrote that having Colbert edit the issue "sort of reeks of desperation more than it does slick PR." And in response to a brief blurb on Politico one commenter, "billp," wrote: "It is sad to see a magazine like *Newsweek* doing this. I like Colbert and I like *Newsweek*, but I don't want a comedian running *Newsweek* anymore than I want strait-laced reporters hosting a 30-min comedy show" (Politico 2003). Several people expressed support for Colbert as guest editor. Ann G (2009), a blogger at No Fact Zone, a Colbert fan site, wrote:

> A slick PR move it may be, but it's one with a purpose. The Iraq war has been virtually forgotten by the media and their ever-dwindling attention span, but it shouldn't be, as long as American troops are still there. I have every confidence in Stephen's ability to both entertain us as "Stephen" and to bring attention to a serious subject that hasn't been getting enough of it.

Some responded to the Colbert Iraq issue with concern that it would trivialize or bias coverage. A *New York Post* writer, for example, wrote: "While there's nothing new to the concept of bringing in a guest editor to edit an issue, some wondered if Meacham was making the right call enlisting a comedian to tackle a sober subject" (Kelly 2009). Several comments on Politico offered snarky indictments of what they saw as *Newsweek*'s unabashed liberal perspective. One commenter, "sad," wrote "Another Obama Kneepad Worshipper . . . yep, that's what Newsweek really needs." Another commenter wrote, "Colbert dry humping Michelle Obama was bad enough to see on TV . . . do we really need to see Colbert dry humping the Obama Administration in WRITING?" And commenter "Jarbee" wrote, "It is called NEWSweek. He needs to change the name if it's some sort of comedy/topical columns mag. I used to trust what they wrote. Less now" (Politico 2003).

The issue was further critiqued according to news norms that privilege individual authorship and ahistoricity when Daily Finance blogger Jeff Bercovici (2009a) chastised Colbert, "you'd think Colbert, as a comedian, might have a little more professional pride than to "borrow" content," demonstrating that he was unaware of the intentional reference Colbert was making to the *Spy* issue. On the *Newsweek* cover is an image of Colbert with "Iraq" spelled in shaved letters on the side of his head. The original *Spy* cover featured an altered image of George Bush Sr. with "The 100" shaved into his head. He later posted the response of *Spy* founders Kurt Andersen and Graydon Carter. Carter said, "It pleased me. And I think we're both relieved that today, as opposed to 1989, America's most entertaining and WASPiest make-believe conservative Republican is the host of a TV show instead of president of the United States" (Bercovici 2009a).

These responses to Colbert's role as guest editor of *Newsweek*, which express concern that it was a marketing ploy, that it trivialized the topic of war and biased the news, reflect a larger anxiety over the increasingly blurred lines separating media genres. In an exchange between Bill Moyers and Jon Stewart, Moyers said: "When I report the news on this broadcast, people say I'm making it up. When you make it up, they say you're telling the truth." Stewart responded, "Yes. Exactly. It's funny. I was talking to Jayson Blair about this. I think we don't make things up. We just distill it to, hopefully, its most humorous nugget. And in that sense it seems faked and skewed just because we don't have to be subjective or pretend to be objective. We can just put it out there" (Moyers 2003).

As Colbert points out, the heart of the tension is that political satire is necessarily about change and news is about neutrality. Satire clashes with professional news norms in that it acknowledges the spectacle. As suggested by the responses to Colbert's issue of *Newsweek* and mainstream news's unsuccessful forays into fake news suggest, people prefer their fake news separate from their real news, without perhaps recognizing the extent to which fake news can augment the news landscape. On his show, for example, Colbert's presentation of the Iraq War and other political issues through the lens of a comedian rather than a journalist allows him to broach topics and embrace perspectives that largely fall outside the realm of journalism. Yet his intentions are straight journalism – to raise awareness of the war.

Fake News from the Outside

"Fake" news being created and presented outside the genres of traditional journalism is expanding political discourse by, as Stewart describes, drawing the attention of the public and journalists to issues and perspectives that are being ignored. When Bill Moyers asked Jon Stewart, "What do you see that journalists don't see?" Stewart replied:

> I think we see exactly what you see, but for some reason, don't analyze it in that manner or put it on the air in that manner. I can't tell you how many times we'll run into a journalist and go, "Boy . . . I wish we could be saying that. That's exactly the way we see it and that's exactly the way we'd like to be saying that." And I always think, "Well, why don't you?" (Moyers 2003)

The Yes Men

Perhaps the most high-profile fakers these days are The Yes Men, Jacque Servin, aka Andy Bichlbaum, and Igor Vamos, aka Mike Bonanno. They describe their role, much like Stewart, as complementing the work of journalists. Mike Bonanno says "we're not making fake news. We're making real news through fakery that's real fake news" (Moyers 2007). In other words they make issues newsworthy by creating spectacles for journalists to cover. They use détournement or what they call "identity correction" in order to highlight the inhumane practices of globalization and to create news hooks so journalists have an excuse to cover an expanded set of issues. Since the late 1990s they have been passing themselves off as people from organizations they don't like, creating websites that appear to be the official sites of politicians, corporations, and governmental organizations in order to gain invitations to represent these entities as official news sources or as conference participants. Once they are given the opportunity to pose as government and corporate spokespeople, they make elaborate presentations and outrageous commentary on the ideology they are critiquing – usually corporate greed fueled by the neoliberal economic practices inspired by economist Milton Friedman. For example, at an International Legal Studies Conference in Salzburg, posing as representatives of the World Trade Organization, Jacque suggested that the siesta should be outlawed, referring to Berlusconi's comments along the same lines, and that people should be able to sell their votes directly to the highest bidder.

Other times they wreak havoc by posing as officials making promises the real officials would never make, bringing to light the constraints of a system that privileges corporate over human interest, and forcing the real officials to publicly explain themselves and their companies' policies. For example, Jacque appeared on the BBC World News posing as "Jude Finisterra," a Dow Chemical spokesman on December 3, 2004, the twentieth anniversary of the Bhopal disaster in which a Dow-owned Union Carbide pesticide plant in India accidentally released methyl isocyanate (MIC). The accident exposed 500,000 people to the poisonous gas, killing an estimated 4,000 people within seventy-two hours. An additional 25,000 people have died since that time from illnesses related to exposure to the gas (Eckerman 2004). On the BBC Finisterra claimed that Dow planned to liquidate Union Carbide and use the resulting $12 billion to pay for medical expenses, clean up the

site, and conduct research into the hazards of other Dow products. After two hours of wide coverage, Dow issued a press release
denying the statement, ensuring even greater coverage of the phony
news of a cleanup. By the time the original story was discredited,
Dow's stock had declined in value by $2 billion (Gilbey 2009).

In an interview with Bill Moyers (2007), Jacque explained that
such pranks help free journalists from the constraints of their
profession.

> We actually see this as a form of journalism. Or perhaps more pre-
> cisely, a form of collaboration with journalists. A lot of the issues that
> we address journalists want to cover. And sometimes it's the reason
> they've gone into journalism. But in many jobs, in many situations,
> editorial control won't let them unless there's a good little hook
> behind it. And so, we've found a way to create funny spectacles that
> give journalists the excuse to cover issues. And sometimes, they work
> really well.

Their hoaxes increasingly directly engage institutions of journalism.
On November 12, 2008, in collaboration with Anti-Advertising
Agency, a group of artists who create works critical of corporate
media, especially advertising, they created 80,000 fake issues of
the *New York Times* dated six months into the future (July 4,
2008) and enlisted volunteers to help hand them out on the streets
of New York, Los Angeles, San Francisco, Chicago, Philadelphia,
and Washington D.C. A press release about the fake edition of the
newspaper read: "It's all about how at this point, we need to push
harder than ever. We've got to make sure Obama and all the other
Democrats do what we elected them to do. After eight, or maybe
twenty-eight years of hell, we need to start imagining heaven."
The above-the-fold headline of the fake edition pronounced
"Iraq War Ends" and the rest of the issue included the announcement of news and initiatives that reflected their idea of what the
paper might look like if it had good news to deliver, including
the establishment of national health care, a maximum wage for
CEOs, a repeal of the Patriot Act, and an indictment of Bush for
treason. The articles were written in traditional news style by three

unnamed *New York Times* reporters and other volunteer journalists. There were also fake advertisements including one from Exxon Mobile, the world's largest publicly traded oil company, saying the company applauded the end of the Iraq War and that peace is "an idea the world can profit from." Another ad from the South African diamond conglomerate De Beers said "your purchase of a diamond will enable us to donate a prosthetic for an African whose hand was lost in diamond conflicts."

Copies of the fake *New York Times* were almost immediately picked up and sold on eBay. And the response on the web and on the street was largely supportive of the hoax. Gawker (2009c), the preeminent Manhattan and beyond gossip rag, wrote, "Well done, sirs. We hope the *Times* doesn't sue you for copyright violations." And Gawker speculated about the aim of the prank and critiqued the fake edition in terms of its effectiveness. The real *New York Times'* measured but positive response to the hoax included a City Room blog post from Sewell Chan, who reported on the issue with the neutral distance of a good newsman. Chan (2008) included a quote from Alex Jones, former *New York Times* reporter and current director of the Joan Shorenstein Center on the Press, Politics and Public Policy at the Harvard Kennedy School, suggesting that the paper should be flattered. He said: "It will probably be a collector's item. I'm just glad someone thinks *The New York Times* print edition is worthy of an elaborate hoax. A Web spoof would have been infinitely easier. But creating a print newspaper and handing it out at subway stations? That takes a lot of effort. I consider this a gigantic compliment to the *Times*."

In another *New York Times* story, Jim Dwyer (2009) calls the fake issue "a Grade-A caper." And judging from the comments posted on the *New York Times* site, readers had an overwhelmingly positive response to the fake issue, with comments like, "You rule the Earth" (Anthro-Pop); and "Only if it were true (or come to be true), then what a wonderful idea/paper this would be" (TwoKad). The story of the spoof edition was posted on highly trafficked sites like Boing Boing and the Huffington Post, and covered in newspapers throughout the U.S., China, India, Germany, Canada, and the U.K. Most of the stories were only a few hundred words, with little or no discussion of the motivations of its creators. A video created by The Yes Men documenting the prank was posted on YouTube (2009) and other video-hosting sites around the web and the prank was featured in the feature-length film *The Yes Men Fix the World*, which was a 2009 official selection of the Sundance Film Festival in 2009 and won the Berlin International Film Festival Audience award, among others.

In fact the only party that seemed rankled by the hoax was De Beers, who, according to the Electronic Frontier Foundation, responded not by confronting the authors (whose parody is protected by the First Amendment) but instead by threatening their Swiss-based domain name registrar, Joker.com. De Beers demanded that Joker.com disable the spoof website's domain name or face liability for trademark infringement (Zimmerman 2008). While De Beers' threats did not result in a takedown of the site, they did ensure that many more people saw the spoof ad.

On September 21, 2009, the day before a UN summit on the climate change in New York, The Yes Men and their network of collaborators and volunteers distributed a "special edition" of the *New York Post* with the headline "We're Screwed" and stories describing the lethal effects on the city of global warming, the U.S. government's apathetic response, and China's advanced alternative energy program. "Although the 32-page *New York Post* is a fake, everything in it is 100% true, with all facts carefully checked by a team of editors and climate change experts. This could be, and should be, a real *New York Post*," said The Yes Men. "Climate change is the biggest threat civilization has ever faced, and it should be in the headlines of every paper, every day until we solve the problem."

This time the reception was not as friendly. Gawker (2009c) commenters complained that it wasn't funny. And while the *New York Post* (2009) claimed it was flattered by the spoof, guards at News Corp building where the *Post* offices are located called on police to confiscate the papers and arrested three volunteers handing out papers outside the building (Bercovici 2009b). In a blog post about the incident in the *New York Times*, David Carr (2009) wrote, "A word to News Corporation news confiscators:

We are in the business of promulgating free speech, not detaining it. Lighten up."

The *Post* spoof received less news coverage than did the spoof of the *New York Times*. The articles and broadcast stories about the *Post* hoax were for the most part brief and contained little in-depth information about the meaning behind the prank. News and commentary about the prank, including the *Post*'s response, circulated widely on the web. Three different versions of the video created by The Yes Men documenting the prank were posted online.

Despite the hostile response from the *Post*, overall The Yes Men say the mainstream media response to their various pranks has been "very nice."

> Mainstream journalists almost always get our serious points, and transmit it to the journalism-consuming consumer. A lot of these people (journalists) really *want* to write about important things – but in the U.S. at least, you can't cover the WTO or the Bhopal anniversary just because they're tremendously important. We can provide the fodder, sometimes, that lets these subjects get covered. (Yes Men n.d.)

The spoof paper and most of The Yes Men's other pranks have been widely covered and the coverage has been mostly sympathetic. On the CNN show *Issues*, the host Jane Velez-Mitchell fawningly showed support for The Yes Men by admitting that she too believed Dow should provide reparations to victims of the Bhopal disaster (YouTube 2009). Their hi-jinks have been documented in two feature-length documentaries, *The Yes Men Movie* (2004) and the previously mentioned *The Yes Men Fix the World* (2009), and the attention they have gained has transformed their strategy from stealthy saboteurs to high-profile critics, working from outside mainstream media institutions to influence their agenda and content. *The Yes Men Fix the World* includes tongue-in-cheek dramatization of the process by which Jacque and Igor orchestrate their pranks – scenes showing the two sitting in squalid conditions in the rubble of an abandoned building creating fake websites and waiting for someone to take the bait so they can conduct a new "identity correction."

Revealing the Aberrations of the Spectacle

The Daily Show skit spoofing the *New York Times* described in the chapter's opening rips the styles and tone of professional journalism and mocks one of the most sacred institutions of the profession. Fake newsman Jason Jones is free to undermine the authority of the elite news media, of course, because he is only *playing* at being a journalist and has no investment in its rules of fairness and no reverence for its institutions. Colbert's editing of *Newsweek* was much more complicated. The appearance of "fake" news in the format and context of the "real" news of *Newsweek* provoked anxiety around the blurring of the genres of news and comedy, which perhaps reflected a broader anxiety about the nature of truth and where it is most likely to be found. News producers and networked publics alike seemed disconcerted by this unholy mixing of genres as funnyman Colbert used satire for the genuine journalistic aims of sparking renewed interest in a serious news item – the Iraq War – an item that had fallen off journalists' radar. At the same time, they seem more tolerant, even celebratory, in response to the pranks of The Yes Men, who, working from the outside of the journalism establishment, created spectacles to influence the "real" news and created "fake" news to shape spectacles.

Megan Boler and Stephen Turpin suggest that a shared frustration and consequent appeal of irony is directly related to a collective attempt at "coping with complacency in spectacular society." They elaborate:

> The appeal of satire and irony is in large part the frank admission of complicity with the spectacle. Beginning with the self assignment of "fake news" (*The Daily Show* is know as "the most trusted name in 'fake news'"), both Jon Stewart and Stephen Colbert instantly assert that their shows are merely comedy and not news, have no partisan agenda, and do not claim to be outside the spectacle of commodity. (2008: 386–7)

Unlike the use of irony in straight news, which Ted Glasser and James Ettema (1998) suggest may lead to cynicism, fake news offers an alternative even as it breaks down the artifice of the spectacle. The alternative is a level of truth that is not found in news, which ignores the existence of the spectacle. As Boler and Turpin argue, even though everyone "knows" the extraordinary lies of spectacle, there remains an enduring desire for truth-telling:

> Demands for accountability arise in response to the flagrant and audacious disregard of politics. . . . However, despite the power maintained by White House, CentCom, and corporate media vectors there is an increasing proliferation of plural narratives, and through the development of digital technologies we see the construction of a public archive that arguably did not exist previously in the public domain as a resource or historical account – e.g., allowing potential of remix, etc. to reveal the aberrations of spectacle as it shapes historical record. (2007: 3)

On October 30, 2010, three days before the U.S. midterm elections, Jon Stewart held the "Rally to Restore Sanity" on the Washington Mall, at once an appeal for more reasonable political discourse and a mockery of the "Rally Restoring Honor," held a few months earlier by conservative radio and television host Glen Beck. The message of that rally was to "get behind the shield of God." Stewart's rally, which merged with partner-in-satire Stephen Colbert's concurrent "March to Keep Fear Alive," created a counter-force to Beck's gathering, and was perhaps the most visible exhibition of engagement and activism associated with fake news icons Colbert and Stewart. The crowd, estimated to be 215,000 strong, bigger than the turnout for Beck's rally, signaled the widespread resonance of these cultural icons and the desire on the part of fans to translate their engagement with the show to engagement with the political realities of the day (Grier 2010).

Here Stewart was remixing a political spectacle and in the process revealing the aberrations of the spectacle. The power of remix does not, of course, rest exclusively in the genre of fake news, but in the way it so effectively exhibits the practice of remixing – taking pieces of dominant culture and rewriting them into alternative narratives. Lawrence Lessig (2008) describes remix culture as a creative work produced by building on the work of the past, and argues that cultural innovation and profitability are tied to the participatory remix process.

This chapter has focused on professional remixers – who, with the occasional exception of The Yes Men pranks, operate largely within the law and the structures of commercial media – in order to demonstrate how remix has become part of the mainstream media landscape while at the same time presenting challenges to it. There are many more examples of political remix created by networked publics, providing additional examples of the re-appropriation of mainstream news materials, formats, and personalities to challenge particular notions of truth and journalism. Video remix can be achieved for little or no cost on home computers and networked publics are using this ability to make powerful political statements. Take, for example, the remix artist Jonathan McIntosh, who creates videos using mainstream media television footage for his raw material in order to make political statements about the government, commercialism, gender politics, and a host of other issues. He describes his work in this way:

> My video work remixes and transforms fragments of mass media pop culture to tell alternative political, social and cultural narratives. Basically I'm a pop culture hacker, but instead of computer code I hack television. My political remixes appear online and also in film festivals, on community tv stations and at new media conferences globally. (McIntosh 2010a)

For example, one widely circulated remix re-creates a military recruitment television commercial with images of torture in Iraq to expose the increasing normalization of torture (McIntosh 2008). An example of what The Yes Men call identity correction, the video mimics the advertisements of powerful institutions in order to change or "correct" their carefully constructed PR image. More recently McIntosh remixed the voice of conservative media pundit Glen Beck with classic Disney Donald Duck cartoons from the 1930s to the 1960s, to create a narrative where Donald's life is turned upside down by economic woes and he finds a seemingly sympathetic voice in Glenn Beck, who spews paranoid and xenophobic rhetoric through the radio (McIntosh 2010b). Beck responded to the remix: "It is some of the best, well-made propaganda I have ever seen. We are looking into the funding of this gentleman and this *incredible* propaganda against me. We'll find out if it's been federally funded – as part of the stimulus package" (YouTube 2010). The fact of the matter is that McIntosh is not funded by the federal government or by anyone at all. He is an independent activist using the fabric of commercial culture to construct new cultural forms and meaning.

Boler (2007) believes that these forms of creative expression that build on the material of dominant culture are a powerful avenue of expression:

> We may not be able to trace an easy "cause and effect" (how do we even separate the producers from consumers in this golden age of user-generated content when all of us have been named person of the year by Time Magazine?). But there can be little doubt that satirists, bloggers, citizen journalists, and YouTube and other viral video producers around the world are taking action daily and dissenting from mainstream media agendas. Whether one traces the effects of Stewart on Crossfire, Colbert at the 2006 White House Press Correspondent's Dinner roasting George W. Bush in front of the President and the world, or blogs that broke the Trent Lott or Rathergate story, the counterpublics created through digital media are far more than water cooler talk. What matters is that dissenting voices are being aired through increasingly broad and multiformat channels. Corporate-owned news and papers of record are being forced to watch their step by the 24/7 surveillance of a vibrant public demanding accountability. The comedians may claim to be only interested in the laugh. But those who watch, think critically, and take numerous forms of action do come away each night with renewed political convictions – not least of which is to question a news media that too often fails in its responsibility to speak truth to power.

Fake news and other forms of political remix both within and outside mainstream outlets represent key components to networked journalism. Not only do they influence news discourse, they signal a larger phenomenon: the evolution of journalistic forms and the emergence of a space for dissent being carved out in the middle of the spectacle. Roughly seventy years after the widespread influence of post-World War II capitalism that created the spectacle the Situationists sought to resist, wariness toward the spectacle is widespread and so are the tools and desire to break it down.

References

Achter, P. (2009) " 'Weekend Update' and the Tradition of New Journalism." Flow, March 21. http://flowtv.org/?p=2966

Ann G. (2009) "Stephen Colbert in the Zeitgeist – Newsweek Preview Edition." No Fact Zone, June 6. http://www.nofactzone.net/2009/06/06/stephen-colbert-in-the-zeitgeist-newsweek preview-edition/

Baym, G. (2005) "The Daily Show: Discursive Integration and the Reinvention of Political Journalism." *Political Communication* 22:3, 259–76.

Benjamin, W. (2001) "Art in the Age of Mechanical Reproduction." In: M.G. Durham & D. Kellner (eds), *Media and Cultural Studies*. New York: Blackwell.

Bercovici, J. (2009a) "Newsweek and Spy: Separated at Birth?" Daily Finance, June 8. http://www.dailyfinance.com/2009/06/08/newsweek-and-spy-separated-at-birth/

Bercovici, J. (2009b) "Activists Behind NY Post Parody Detained by Police." Daily Finance, September 21. http://www.dailyfinance.com/2009/09/21/activists-behind-ny-post-parody-detained-by-police/#comment

Boler, M. (2007) "Changing the World One Laugh at a Time: The Daily Show and Political Activism." Counter Punch, February 20. http://www.counterpunch.org/boler02202007.html

Boler, M. & Turpin, S. (2007) "Ironic Citizenship, or Coping with Complicity in Spectacular Society." New Network Culture Theory Conference, Amsterdam June http://www.meganboler.net/publications/#EssaysChapters

Boler, M. & Turpin, S. (2008) "The Daily Show and Crossfire: Satire and Sincerity as Truth to Power." In: M. Boler (ed.), *Digital Media and Democracy: Tactics in Hard Times*. Cambridge, MA: MIT Press.

Boljanovic, S. (2007) "Croatia: 'Feral Tribune' Shuts Down." Global Voices Online, June 20. http://globalvoicesonline.org/2007/06/20/croatia-feral-tribune-shuts-down/

Carr, D. (2009) "New York Post Parody Detained." *New York Times*, September 22. http://mediadecoder.blogs.nytimes.com/2009/09/22/ny-post-parody-detained/

Chan, S. (2008) "Liberal Pranksters Hand Out Times Spoof." *New York Times*, November 12. http://www.cityroom.blogs.nytimes.com/2008/11/12/pranksters-spoof-the-times/

Colbert, S. (2006) "A Conversation with Stephen Colbert." Political Humor Series, Harvard University's Institute of Politics JFK Forum, http://video.google.com/videoplay?docid=5550134133036374310#

Debord, G. (1967) *The Society of the Spectacle.* Exeter: Revel Press.

Debord, G. (2001) "Commodity and Spectacle." In: M.G. Durham and D. Kellner (eds), *Media and Cultural Studies.* New York: Blackwell.

Delli Carpini, M.X. & Williams, B.A. (2001) "Let us Infotain You: Politics in the New Media Environment." In: W.L. Bennett & R.M. Entman (eds), *Mediated Politics: Communication in the Future of Democracy.* New York: Cambridge University Press.

Deveny, K. (2009) "Reinventing Newsweek." *Newsweek*, May 18. http://www.newsweek.com/id/195620

Druick, Z. (2009) "Dialogic Absurdity: TV News Parody as a Critique of Genre." *Television and New Media* 10, 294.

Dwyer, J. (2009) "Today's Paper." *New York Times*, July 7. http://www.nytimes-se.com/2009/07/04/todays-paper

Eckerman, I. (2004) *The Bhopal Saga: Causes and Consequences of the World's Largest Industrial Disaster.* Hyderabad: Universities Press.

Feral Tribune (2007) http://www.ex-yupress.com/feral/feralindex.html

Gawker (2009a) "Thinky New Newsweek Bringing on Stephen Colbert as Guest Editor." June 3. http://gawker.com/5276724/thinky-new-newsweek-bringing-on-stephen-colbert-as-guest-editor

Gawker (2009b) "The Daily Show Goes to Visits the New York Times, Purveyors of Aged News." June 11. http://gawker.com/5286813/the-daily-show-visits-the-new-york-times-purveyors-of-aged-news

Gawker (2009c) "The Fake *New York Post*: Get Yours Now." September 21. http://gawker.com/5364046/the-fake-new-york-post-get-yours-now

Gilbey, R. (2009) "Jokers to the Left, Jokers to the Right." *Guardian*, July 17.

Glasser, T. & Ettema, J. (1998) *Custodians of Conscious.* New York: Columbia University Press.

Goodman, M. (2008) *The Sun and the Moon: The Remarkable True Account of Hoaxers, Showmen, Dueling Journalists, and Lunar Man-Bats in Nineteenth-Century New York.* New York: Basic Books.

Gray, J., Jones, J., & Thompson E. (2009) *Satire TV: Politics and Comedy in the Post-Network Era.* New York: NYU Press.

Grier, P (2010) "Jon Stewart's Rally Attendance: Really Bigger than Glen Beck's?" *Christian Science Monitor*, 1 November. http://www.csmonitor.com/USA/Election-2010/Vox-News/2010/1101/Jon-Stewart-rally-attendance-Really-bigger-than-Glenn-Beck-s

Jenkins, H. (2002) "Interactive Audiences?" In: Don Harris (ed.), *The New Media Book.* London: British Film Institute.

Jenkins, H. (2005) *Convergence Culture: Where Old and New Media Collide.* New York: NYU Press.

Johnson, S. (2009) "Stephen Colbert as Newsweek Guest Editor: What Should We Expect?" *Chicago Tribune*, June 5. http://articles.chicagotribune.com/2009-06-05/news/0906040874_1_newsweek-guest-editor-readers

Jones, J. (2004) "Entertaining Politics." In: L. van Zoonen (ed.), *Entertaining the Citizen: When Politics and Popular Culture Converge.* New York: Rowman & Littlefield Publishers, Inc.

Jones, J. (2007) "'Fake News' versus 'Real' News as Sources of Political Information: *The Daily Show* and Postmodern Political Reality." In: K. Riegert (ed.), *Politicotainment: Television's Take on the Real.* New York: Peter Lang.

Kalin, M. (2006) "Why Jon Stewart Isn't Funny." *Boston Globe*, March 3. http://www.boston.com/ae/movies/oscars/articles/2006/03/03/why_jon_stewart_isnt_funny/

Kelly, K.J. (2009) "Weekly's 'Truthiness': Colbert to Guest Edit Newsweek Issue." *New York Post*, June 4. http://www.nypost.com/seven/06042009/business/weeklys_truthiness_172439.htm

Koblin, J. (2009) "Bottom of Form Newsweek Turns to Tina Tricks: Meet Guest Editor . . . Stephen Colbert!" *New York Observer*, June 2. http://www.observer.com/2009/media/newsweek-turns-tina-tricks-meet-guest-editor-%E2%80%A6-stephen-colbert

LaMarre, H.L., Landreville, Kristen D., & Beam, M.A. (2009) "The Irony of Satire: Political Ideology and the Motivation to See What You Want to See in *The Colbert Report.*" *The International Journal of Press/Politics* 14:2, 212–31.

Lessig, L. (2008) *Remix: Making Art and Commerce Thrive in a Hybrid Economy.* New York: Penguin Press.

McDonough, T. (2007) *The Beautiful Language of My Century: Reinventing the Language of Contestation in Postwar France, 1945–1968.* Cambridge, MA: MIT Press.

McIntosh, J. (2008) "Go Army: Bad Guys." Rebellious Pixels, August 19. http://www.rebelliouspixels.com/2008/go-army-bad-guys

McIntosh, J. (2010a) "About Jonathan McIntosh." Rebellious Pixels. http://rebelliouspixels.com/about-jonathan-mcintosh

McIntosh, J. (2010b) "Donald Duck Meets Glenn Beck in Right Wing Radio Duck." Rebellious Pixels, October 2. http://www.rebelliouspixels.com/2010/right-wing-radio-duck-donald-discovers-glenn-beck

Manovich, L. (2001) *The Language of New Media.* Cambridge, MA: MIT Press.

Meacham, J. (2009) "A Reader's Guide to the Colbert Issue." *Newsweek*, June 6. http://www.newsweek.com/id/200857?tid=relatedcl

Meikle, G. (2008) "Whacking Bush." In: M. Boler (ed.), *Digital Media and Democracy: Tactics in Hard Times.* Cambridge, MA: MIT Press.

Miller, P. (2004) *Rhythm Science Audio Companion: Excerpts and Allegories from the Sub Rosa Archives.* Cambridge, MA: Mediaworks.

Moyers, B. (2003) Transcript Bill Moyers Interviews Jon Stewart. July 11. http://www.pbs.org/now/transcript/transcript_stewart.html

Moyers, B. (2007) Bill Moyers Journal Transcript. July 20. http://www.pbs.org/moyers/journal/07202007/transcript4.html

New York Post (2009) "We're Flattered! Fake 'Post' Prank." September 22. http://www.nypost.com/p/news/local/we_re_flattered_fake_post_prank_5ReZ weJX60raS1Oj8S8GDP#ixzz0WlStviNj

Pew (2009) "Press Accuracy Rating Hits Two Decade Low: Public Evaluations of the News Media: 1985–2009." The Pew Research Center for People and the Press. http://people-press.org/report/543/

Politico (2003) Readers' comment to Michael Calderone's comment on Politico, "Newsweek's First Guest Editor: Colbert." http://www.politico.com/blogs/ michaelcalderone/0609/Newsweeks_first_guest_editor_Colbert.html#

Tribble, S. (2008) *A Colossal Hoax: The Giant from Cardiff That Fooled America*. New York: Rowman & Littlefield Publishers, Inc.

Yes Men (n.d.) The Yes Men Frequently Asked Questions. http://theyesmen.org/ faq

YouTube (2009) "Fake NY Times Hoax on CNN (The Yes Men)." http://www. youtube.com/watch?v=dO6Oi3XUYgg

YouTube (2010) "Insider Video of Glenn Beck Responding to Donald Duck Remix Video." http://www.youtube.com/watch?v=1ytW917TBI8

Zimmerman, M. (2008) "Censorship in the 21st Century: Targeting Intermediaries." Electronic Frontier Foundation, November 25. http://www. eff.org/deeplinks/2008/11/de-beers-internet-intermediaries

5

Public Life and the Future of News

When someone demands to know how we are going to replace newspapers, they are really demanding to be told that we are not living
through a revolution.

Clay Shirky (2009)

The last decade and a half has been host to countless discussions
on the future of news. There was a Congressional hearing. There
have been conferences, community gatherings, industry meetings,
white papers, articles, books, and speeches, all of which arrive
with an increasing sense of urgency. Journalists and others concerned with democracy and public life seek signs of the future in
the recent history of journalism and the emerging shape of digital
news. Too many of these discussions, however, conflate saving the
news industry with saving journalism.

There is little doubt that the news industry is failing, many
believe irrevocably. In 2009 cable and online news were the only
media with audience growth. National and local broadcast news,
magazines, and newspapers continued to lose revenue and audience. Every commercial news media sector saw revenue declines
except for cable television (Pew 2010). The financial deteriora-
tion of newspapers in the United States has been especially rapid
and dramatic. Between 2008 and 2009 newspaper industry woes
reached a peak as profits fell and management tried to cut costs
by cutting reporting staff and eliminating Saturday press runs,
among other things. Newspaper chains and individually owned

papers struggled, declared bankruptcy, and shuttered in cities such as Denver, Seattle, Tucson, and Kansas City. There's no shortage of theories about why this has been the case. We want conversations not lectures (Rosen 2006). We trust each other more than we trust journalists and politicians (Purcell et al. 2010). Digital Craigslist killed classified ads (Glaser 2004). Declining social capital and civic life diminished appetites for serious journalism (Putnam 2000). News industry hubris hobbled the will to adapt to emergent conditions. As prolific author and consultant Clay Shirky (2009) puts it:

> The curious thing about the various plans hatched in the '90s is that they were, at base, all the same plan: "Here's how we're going to preserve the old forms of organization in a world of cheap perfect copies!" The details differed, but the core assumption behind all imagined outcomes . . . was that the organizational form of the newspaper, as a general-purpose vehicle for publishing a variety of news and opinion, was basically sound, and only needed a digital facelift.

The digital facelifts with their computer-generated links and non-search-friendly headlines and paywalls and staid unsharable videos failed to make the newspaper news product any more desirable to growing swaths of the public. Yet the networked public continues to devour information at rates news moguls of the past wouldn't dare to imagine (Purcell at al. 2010). The people formerly known as news consumers want more news and they want to be able to do more with it.

Publishers and media entrepreneurs have so far failed to successfully address this problem head on as a business challenge. Analysts across disciplines have understandably stepped into the breach and led the way in exploring larger related themes to which news industry people have gravitated. Mostly they lament the coming death of accountability journalism and warn against a rising tide of corrupted power certain to follow (McChesney & Nichols 2010); and they argue that the coming fragmented media landscape will heighten societal polarization as we isolate ourselves in communication silos that merely reflect our own beliefs and interests, making us less willing and less able to understand alternative views and to sympathize with those who hold them (Sunstein 2002) – both well-founded concerns. Placed at the center of debates concerning the future of journalism, however, they have skewed the discussion, steering it away from a more relevant question raised by the networked activity that characterizes this transitional moment and marks it off as different from the past. The question today is how to build a future that caters to the deeper engagement with information demonstrated on a mass scale every minute of every day in the networked era. The question is how to cater to and harness best the awe-inspiring energy digitally connected humans pour into information generating, tweaking, interpreting and sharing. It seems to me that admittedly important concerns about the future of accountability journalism and the risks of social polarization will be addressed as the answer to this larger, more immediate question emerges. The value of amateur war reporting, citizen journalism projects, WikiLeaks data dumps, ironic and satirical journalism, for example – the phenomena I have presented in this book – rises when they are evaluated based on the level and quality of engagement they foster. It is the engagement that compels when considering the emerging media landscape. How exactly do they foster engagement? What kind of engagement do they foster? What can be done with this or that kind of engagement? Innovative and promising projects have gone unremarked upon in discussions about the future of news because they don't fit into the traditional categories that mark out the conversations. A dynamic networked journalism landscape may come not by merely seeking to save the news industry but by exploring the elements of emergent communication most likely to facilitate vibrant and participatory publics.

News industry upheaval is occurring just as new possibilities are emerging. New conceptions of the public are creating new spaces for participation in the newsmaking process, even as professional journalism outlets struggle to maintain authority. The shift from personalization to socialization and the technology that support this more sophisticated two-way exchange is creating journalism that is more collaborative and journalism product that is more malleable. Journalism as multimedia storytelling and multi-genre material has likewise expanded and the news environment in its production and sourcing and distribution is less hierarchical and uniform. The popularity of "fake" journalism like *The Daily Show* fosters increased "ironic citizenship" that is both an antidote to and a product of the networked-era news transition.

There is a central tension between a journalism in which professionals are considered exclusively qualified to discover and distribute the news, on one hand, and a journalism in which the public is involved in creating, circulating, and critiquing the news, on the other. Those journalisms depend on different sets of tools and practices. There is no dominant new model. As is painfully apparent to people in the newspaper industry, long-standing business models and professional infrastructure are deteriorating quicker than new ones are being built. Denial, as Shirky (2009) writes, has been an understandable reaction:

> When someone demands to know how we are going to replace newspapers, they are really demanding to be told that we are not living through a revolution. They are demanding to be told that old systems won't break before new systems are in place. They are demanding to be told that ancient social bargains aren't in peril, that core institutions will be spared, that new methods of spreading information will improve previous practice rather than upending it.

Complicating reactions to the changes, however, is the fact that journalism now includes experimental projects being run both inside and outside the industry, projects that are both extending and replacing systems and social bargains. There is no consensus at this point even on how to measure success. Certainly much of the denial Shirky refers to comes as a result of confusion over whether we are living through an evolution or a revolution. Yet on the ground each day to greater and lesser degrees we are remaking journalism, a fact that begs the question: What kind of journalism should we be trying to make?

An Essential Resource

In a democracy, an order built on the public, a free press is fundamental, because a public tasked with governing itself has to have access to information and freedom of expression. The vast majority of stakeholders in the debate over the future of journalism agree to that much. Beyond that threshold, opinions diverge, including opinions on what constitutes a free press and what conditions are necessary to sustain it. One of the most contentious strains of debate in the United States about journalism in transition is to what extent the government should become involved in supporting it. The Knight Commission on the Information Needs of Communities in a Democracy recently declared journalism "as vital to the healthy functioning of communities as clean air, safe streets, good schools and public health." U.S. Senator Ben Cardin introduced legislation in 2009 to grant newspapers non-profit status, which includes tax breaks, but the bill failed to gain support in part because it offered no solutions to how non-viable businesses can be converted to viable non-profits. Robert McChesney and John Nichols argue that before deregulation and the hyper-commercialization of the news industry in the 1980s (2009, 2010), journalism was not only seen as a public good, but was heavily subsidized by the government through tax breaks, postal subsidies, and the printing of public notices.

> Only a nihilist would consider it sufficient to rely on profit-seeking commercial interests or philanthropy to educate our youth or defend the nation from attack. With the collapse of the commercial news system, the same logic applies. Just as there came a moment when policymakers recognized the necessity of investing tax dollars to create a public education system to teach our children, so a moment has arrived at which we must recognize the need to invest tax dollars to create and maintain news gathering, reporting and writing with the purpose of informing all our citizens. (McChesney & Nichols 2009)

The case made by McChesney and Nichols for the "public option" has failed to gain wide traction mainly due to concerns that a government that pays for the press will control the press. The public option also suffers because it romanticized the past and aims to sustain a mass-media model dominant for deades that might be better replaced. Supporting the hierarchical and insular newspaper model with its tiers of editors and teams of beat reporters might well not be the most effective way to deliver valuable journalism. If we agree with the argument that journalism at its best seeks to keep power in check, for instance, then we have to examine the potential of new projects that combine traditional accountability journalism with the speed, reach, low cost, and wide authorship afforded by networked tools.

The Public's Right to Know

In a widely read 2009 report entitled "The Reconstruction of American Journalism," Michael Schudson and Leonard Downie, Jr. acknowledge that mass-media accountability journalism is threatened by the decline of newspapers, but they also recognize the potential of networked-media developments: "[D]igital technology – joined by innovation and entrepreneurial energy – is opening new possibilities for reporting. Journalists can research much more widely, update their work repeatedly, follow it up more thoroughly, verify it more easily, compare it with that of competitors, and have it enriched and fact-checked by readers." More significantly perhaps, the "new possibilities" opened up for reporting are not just opened up to people we think of today as journalists. "Fake news" anchors, gossip bloggers, and amateurs everywhere unafraid of offending their subjects or burning sources and unconstrained by newsroom editors and publishers run hard with information made available on the web. Indeed, one of the biggest accountability stories of 2009 was delivered by WikiLeaks, the extra-national organization that draws in and posts to the web internal and confidential corporate and government memos and other damning documents of all sorts. In April, WikiLeaks posted classified video of an American military helicopter attack on civilians in Iraq that was distributed far and wide, forcing news organizations to report on the event and officials to comment. The video raised discussion among the public about war in general, the War on Terrorism and the Iraq War in particular, and about U.S. military culture and culpability in civilian injury and death. Levels of accountability spiraled in every direction from the leak. In the case of the Washington Post, it seems clear that WikiLeaks forced the editors to run new reporting on the story as it slowly came out that the paper had been sitting on the same video for a year (Greenwald 2010b).

Journalists and editors at the top U.S. news outlets covered the information available through WikiLeaks in major in-depth pieces that were accompanied with some edit notes expressing wariness about the WikiLeaks project. That wariness didn't amount to much, the thin editorial protests outdone by the stories produced with the WikiLeaks information a thousandfold. The information was blockbuster political material and it was being covered at first by the major competition and then by everyone else. In 2010 Wikileaks posted three "megaleaks" for the internet public but delivered the same information in advance to mainstream news organizations, which helped to verify, archive, and report on the documents. In July came the Afghan War Diary, a collection of internal U.S. military logs documenting civilian casualties and increased Taliban attacks, and generally painting a picture of a grim, plodding operation with no clear resolution in sight. In October came the Iraq War Logs, a cache of more than 400,000 classified military documents, referred to by the German daily *Der Spiegel* as "the greatest data leak in U.S. military history." In November WikiLeaks teamed with *El País*, *Le Monde*, *Der Spiegel*, the U.K. *Guardian*, and the *New York Times* to begin releasing 261 of more than 250,000 confidential U.S. diplomatic cables. The documents included unguarded comments about diplomatic and counter-intelligence operations and backroom gossip about world leaders. Despite attempts by the U.S. government to criminalize WikiLeaks founder Julian Assange and others associated with the WikiLeaks project (Walker 2010) and assertions reported widely in the mainstream media that the released documents amounted to an attack on the U.S. government and a threat to U.S. military personnel (Leonard 2010), Assange won an Amnesty International Media Award in 2009 and was named Readers' Choice for *Time* magazine's Person of the Year in 2010. All of the leaked documents were subsequently authenticated and mainstream news outlets the world over justify their role in disseminating the documents by citing the public's right to information (Greenwald 2010a). Political analysts also argued that the window into government affairs provided by the documents acted to prod publics into making change. They point as examples to Tunisia and Egypt, where in early 2011 citizens took to the streets and overthrew their government whose corrupt leaders, in both cases, were featured in documents posted by WikiLeaks (Dickinson 2011). Critics and champions of WikiLeaks agree that it emerged in 2010 as one of the most influential new-media ventures in the world, a government watchdog media organization on a new transnational scale, free of the constraints of editors, publishers, government officials, and even publishing page-space. Barring a national or coordinated international government attack on the organization, WikiLeaks plans to use its global network of volunteers and servers to release millions more documents in the future from world governments and corporations.

Imagined Communities

Another valued quality of traditional journalism many consider threatened by the rise of networked media is the ability of mass media to foster what Benedict Anderson (1983) called "imagined communities," where audience members perceived themselves to be a part of a group beyond their everyday lives, to identify as part of a city, state, national community, because that's how they were being addressed. Journalism, the thinking goes, forms publics by providing a foundation of shared information, values, and even ritual from which, among other things, to shape governance. James Carey argued that "reading a newspaper [in this view is seen less] as sending or gaining information and more as attending a mass, a situation in which nothing new is learned but in which a particular view of the world is portrayed and confirmed" (1989:

138

20). Ted Glasser (2000) points to a study by Bernard Berelson of the 1945 New York newspaper delivery strikes, where Berelson wrote that what people missed about the newspaper was the routine that accompanied reading it and talking to other New Yorkers about what they read. The newspaper strike created not only an informational void but also a social void in the comfort that comes of exchanging opinions on shared knowledge. The concern is that in the networked era, where each of us has the ability to round up our own information, we will share less and our values and areas of knowledge will diverge, our differences intensified as we choose between information "silos" where we read and hear and watch only things that build on what we know and that reaffirm the values we possess. Yet that concern already seems to be thinning as networked-information consuming habits come increasingly into focus.

Strong communities are clearly being built on the web around journalism information, questions about the nature and activity of those communities begging additional research. Interactive participation in producing the news as well as in filtering and aggregating and commenting upon it – the kind of participation apparent on networks such as Reddit, for example – may well create a comparably higher population of citizens that is comparably more committed to its imagined communities. In any case, the networked media environment, so far, does not seem to have thinned the binding quality of mainstream mediated culture in the United States, where millions tune into Fox News and *The Daily Show* every day and take to the internet to dish about the shows and the topics of the shows and to build new information and cultural products that depend on knowledge of the originals. Whatever critics may say about the politically left and right "silos" of information and opinion represented, for example, by the Huffington Post and MSNBC on one side and the Drudge Report and Fox News on the other, they can't accurately say that the two sides do not share common topics of debate and subjects of interest or data to be analyzed or at least spun. Indeed, for better or for worse, these highly trafficked outlets set the hourly news cycle.

More to the point, the emergent forms of journalism presented in this book include community building spurred by new forms of participation. Of course, public engagement with the news is not a priority unique to the networked era. The ability to circulate and engage with news opinion and information has been understood as a fundamental right for centuries, one that accompanied the rise of philosophies of democracy and was enshrined in founding government documents like the U.S. Constitution. In 1948, Article 19 of the United Nations Universal Declaration of Human Rights (UDHR) lifted access to information to new formal heights: "Everyone has the right to freedom of opinion and expression; this right includes freedom to hold opinions without interference and to seek, receive and impart information and ideas through any media and regardless of frontiers." Those lofty words, taken for granted in the West decades after the Cold War, take on new relevance in the internet era. In the mass-media era, relatively few people could practice or did practice direct journalism. We accepted representative journalism. More than that, we accepted the fact that the public interest would be represented by an increasingly corporate and professionalized news culture characterized by a strong separation between those on the inside and those on the outside. John Hartly sees the United Nations declaration on journalism as a human right call to action rather than a statement of fact (2008: 45). He doesn't believe the internet alone will create a new more direct form of journalism, a good he believes is worth consciously working to achieve. He believes news audiences have to be encouraged to move beyond what he calls the "reading public" developed and extended by journalism in past centuries toward a "writing public" invested in achieving full "read–write literacy," where everyone is a journalist and everyone has the right and access to the means to create and circulate journalistic information and opinions. "So-called user-led innovation will reinvent journalism," he writes, "bringing it closer to the aspirational ideal of a right for everyone" (2008: 50).

The Future: *New Players, New Functions, New Truths*

New Players, New Functions

As I have underlined in this book – by shedding light on the burgeoning number and variety of contributions to the contemporary
field of journalism made by, for example, amateurs and satirists
and niche beat reporters working across media – "journalist"
today is a contested term, a term that still bestows legitimacy and
access and that is being reworked on the ground, partly by business and labor realities. The gloomy statistics reflecting realities
are familiar to news industry watchers. The American Society
of News Editors reported (2009) that in 2008 U.S. dailies shed
5,900 out of roughly 52,200 total newsroom jobs, an 11.3 percent
reduction in the newspaper industry editorial workforce. It was
the largest one-year decline ever and double the decline of the year
before. The peak year in newsroom staffing came nearly a decade
earlier, in 2001, when newspapers employed 56,400 newsroom
staff, roughly the time, as I argue in the introduction to this book,
that represents the culmination of the mass-media era. In the years
since then, the contours of the industry and the profession have
grown as cloudy for members of the profession as they have for
analysts and the public. Indeed, many of the journalists I talked to
in conducting the research for this book casually question whether
what they are doing today is in fact journalism. Denis Burgierman,
for example, wrote to me about what he has been doing since he
returned to Brazil after a year-long Knight Foundation journalism
fellowship at Stanford University. He wasn't sure how to catego-
rize some of his media activities:

> I've been involved in a collaborative public intervention we're doing
> in an alley here in Sao Paulo. It started with a magazine (an independ-
> ent publication called Gotas (http://gotas2.wordpress.com/). In the
> magazine's first issue we wrote that we wanted the second one to have
> a real impact in the city. We invited readers to send ideas and donate
> their work. Now there are about thirty of us and we are . . . trying

141

to reinvigorate an alley in the city. The next issue of Gotas will be to register and document this action. Is this "journalism-related"? I'm not sure. But it is definitely cool. (Unpublished correspondence with author 2010)

Long-time tech and business San Francisco journalist Jeff Davis, editor at Bizmore.com, was similarly unclear on and unconcerned with categorizing his recent work:

I'm helping create the equivalent of Techmeme for an executive/ business audience on the Web. What you say?
   Techmeme is a site that aggregates the feeds from thousands of tech blogs and other web sources around related tech topics. At Bizmore, we're starting to do that for a wildly disaggregated universe of business and management blogs and other sources – and use a combination of human filtering and algorithms to produce a stream of high quality content that businesspeople would otherwise have to go out and find on their own. OK so maybe not journalism related, per se, but I think it's web 2.0 tools like these that give power to more and more citizen journalists. (It's also an alternative to relying solely on Google.) The demand out there is for relevant content; the audience is agnostic as to the source. Bye bye, big media. You get the idea. (Unpublished correspondence with author 2010)

Kevin Molony, freelance photojournalist and *New York Times* contributor, says long-established ideas about staffing at big media projects are changing fast:

I am sure it's all going freelance. No matter what happens in the fortunes of historic media, there will be a dwindling number of staff jobs for news gatherers. In their place, individual freelancers or collectives of reporters and photographers, such as Global Post and Luceo Images, will take up the newsgathering alongside free work from citizen aficionados of a subject. (Unpublished correspondence with author 2010)

Kevin Anderson, formerly of the U.K. *Guardian* and the BBC, puts it this way: "There will be more of us committing random acts of journalism, but there will be fewer of us getting paid to do journalism, at least in the traditional sense of reporting and writing stories" (unpublished correspondence with author 2010).

Mark Deuze has extensively documented these trends in his book *Media Work*, in which he argues that the new, more fluid employment patterns of media professionals allow for innovation in the field: "To some extent this has opened up the creative process in the media for technological and economical interventions, particularly regarding the flexibilization of work and the individual autonomy of media professionals" (2007: 82). Kevin Anderson echoes this sentiment when he describes leaving the *Guardian*:

> I leave institutions wishing that I could have done more but also realizing that I did about as much as I could have. Institutions always have an inbuilt bias to self-preservation, which creates a brake on innovation. I realised that most of my ideas now would never happen in an institution, but I believe that to create a future for journalism, I needed a space to try and test these ideas. (Unpublished correspondence with author 2010)

Most journalists will no longer work exclusively for one media organization and many will work without the security of knowing where their next paycheck will come from and without job basics such as health insurance and professional benefits such as event press passes and the protection afforded by shield laws (Deuze 2007). Increasing numbers of the class of people formerly working as unhyphenated journalists will join the ranks of hyphenated journalists: the citizen-, amateur-, freelance-, comedian-, celebrity-journalists, and so on. They will also compete with the journalists who don't go by that name at all: the WikiLeakers, gossips, video mashup artists, activists, politicians, community organizers, web developers and others. Gabor Vajda, chief correspondent for one of the most highly trafficked Hungarian-language news portals, index.hu, likens this transition period in journalism to the rise of air travel:

> Railway companies had a hegemony for a long time as far as transportation goes, but when air travel became feasible, and later widespread, no one really expected engine drivers to retrain as pilots and railway

companies to transform into airlines. The task remained the same (carrying people and goods) but the entire paradigm changed and new players appeared – I think the same is true for journalism, whether we like it or fear it. (Unpublished correspondence with author 2010)

As has been outlined throughout the book, new players, tools, and economic conditions demand new skills in the emergent environment. Most notable, perhaps, the abundance of information now available creates a need for community organizers and information architects, people who know how to bring together publics around particular topics and how to best sift material. These new-style newsroom professionals will work to facilitate dialogue in a way that makes newspaper letters to the editor pages seem an even more quaint unserious afterthought than they seem today.

Many news organization and independent journalism platforms are actively working to build community around their product as a way of building loyal readers and to increase the power and efficacy of their news and information products. Aron Pilhofer, Editor of Interactive News Technologies at the *New York Times*, points out that the paper is host to several different communities that support a two-way conversation among journalists and networked publics and that create filters to help audiences sort through material. These projects lean on journalists and their readers as not only sources of information and opinion but also references for other related media content. Salon.com's social networking platform has been consciously transformed into a hub of audience activity. Salon.com Editor in Chief Kerry Lauerman said the intention of building Open Salon was to "activate our audience and really turn them into publishing partners" (unpublished correspondence with author 2010).

Online communities have long been a central part of non-commercial and activist media projects. An international community developed around listserv news and information about the Zapatista movement in Mexico in the 1990s. Local communities gather around the Independent Media websites. User communities have developed on YouTube (Wesch 2008), and, more recently, Twitter and Facebook users foster community around topics and shared interests as a central activity. It is only recently that news outlets have started to see value in community building and community maintenance as an essential component of their product and of the work of journalism.

This community building is part of a larger response to the problem networked-era critics see arising from the unruly and ever-expanding sea of digital information. Shirky writes that we are not experiencing an information overload but a "filter failure." We know what to do with scarcity; we scrimp and save until we've made it through. But we get lost in abundance; it distracts us and makes us feel overwhelmed (Shirky 2009). In order to manage the abundance, therefore, journalism will need to give more centrality to the role of community building as filter.

Journalism is also expanding in terms of whose voices are included. Projects meant to create community among readers like Open Salon and the *New York Times* issue-related blogs, as well as spaces carved out online strictly to host reader–writer aggregator-communities such as Reddit, greatly expand perspectives. The debate on these can be furious and highly entertaining and full of insight. More than that, though, the debate signals the desire on the part of networked publics to engage and to represent themselves and shape the stories and interpretation of stories presented. Leveraging the network can have great practical value when, for example, crowdsourcing is used to access information that enhances our understanding of news event and issues.

One dazzling example of the practical uses of crowdsourcing is Ushahidi (meaning testimony in Swahili), a suite of crisis reporting tools first used after the post-election violence in Kenya at the beginning of 2007. The site used SMS and geo-location tools to collect and map mobile phone reports of election-related violence and other human rights violations. Ushahidi was built with open-source software so others are free to adapt and use it to match varying contexts. And they have. Mission 4636 used Ushihidi during the aftermath of the 2010 Haiti earthquake to gather location information about trapped victims. With the help of Crowdflower, a crowdsource application that allowed volunteers to translate messages from Creole to English, messages were mapped, translated, prioritized, and sent on to the coastguard for emergency response. Al-Jazeera used Ushihidi to collect reports and map events related to the war in Gaza. Ryan Ozimek, founder and CEO of open source web-development firm Picnet, used Ushahidi during the 2010 blizzard in Washington, D.C. Ozimek told *Wired* magazine:

> No offense to the hard-working government workers doing their best to help clean up the city, but I was tired of seeing my streets clogged with snow, and neighbors stuck inside. So, I thought I'd start a little website yesterday afternoon to help connect people having snowmageddon problems – say, a stuck car – with people that have snowmageddon solutions, like strong arms and a shovel. (Van Buskirk 2010)

Kevin Anderson describes this distributed networked news gathering as a clear resource for generating information in a crisis as well as for "breaking new ground in organizing literally thousands of people around the world to work on highly technical projects and to solve challenging problems around verification in some of the most challenging conditions, such as after the earthquake in Haiti" (unpublished correspondence with author 2010). The *New York Times* reporter Anand Gitidharadas (2010) notes that a lot can go wrong with this model but that the tendency is to correct through averages by encouraging greater participation. "People could lie, get addresses wrong, exaggerate their situation. But as data collects, crisis maps can reveal underlying patterns of reality: How many miles inland did the hurricane kill? Are the rapes broadly dispersed or concentrated near military barracks." Patrick Meier, director of the crisis map operation says, "We're moving beyond the idea that information is completely true or false" (Gitidharadas 2010).

New Truths

This idea that information is not completely true or false radically departs from the view of truth on which professional journalism has been built. Journalists, as the received wisdom of the professional culture goes, uncover the truth about issues and events by following certain procedures and rules, by, for example, getting two sides of the story to create balance, gathering information from bureaucratically credible sources, and, above all, remaining objective by separating fact from value when conveying the story to the public (Schudson 2003). Indeed truth has been the main product journalists have had to offer. It has been the end product of their craft. While trust used to be based on faith in a journalist's ability to remain neutral, in the era of networked journalism overflowing with opinion, information, and new-style news amateur products, trust is based on transparency, on the links to source material, and on whether the reporter has established a track record of just plain "getting it right" (Rosen 2009).

The information that emerges from the sea of truths and non-truths generated on Ushahidi that Meier refers to can be seen as a metaphor for the larger web. Ushahidi users get valuable information from the crowd because they have learned to read the maps and find from them what they need. So too, on the web, networked publics gain the ability to identify valuable information and call out bad information, which in the end will likely prove more reliable than simply trusting mainstream media outlets and their professionals based on belief in the brand and the promise of objectivity. As the web matures, a set of quality and ethical standards will emerge that will aid in our ability to find and produce reliable information. Jay Rosen (2009) suggests a set of steps that will ensure reliability: "Tell the truth, know what you are talking about, here's where I am coming from, this is the best we could do right now, (when new info comes in I'll update), what do you know that I don't and you consistently follow those ethics the result will be you will become reliable." Audiences will come to demand accuracy and transparency, according to Rosen, because there will always be people who know more about the topic under discussion than the "journalist" reporting it, only now these experts will be connected to the story and able to directly comment on it and alter its meanings. People who know more can now find the news writers and find the news writers' readers and they can call out inaccuracies and misreadings in near real time at the site where the material was published, making their critique a part of the story.

Strengthening Networked Publics

Jessica Clark and Pat Aufderheide report that "after a decade of quick-fire innovation – first Web pages, then interactive Flash sites, first blogs, then Twitter, first podcasts, then iPhones; first DVDs, then BitTorrent – the individual has moved from being an anonymous part of a mass to being the center of the media picture" (2009: 5). The American University's Center for Social Media has extensively documented the trends in public media in a series of reports and offers concrete suggestions on how to move forward to create next-generation public media, because, as they put it, "[it] won't happen by accident." They anticipate that the same market imperative that drives news media today will shape the media of tomorrow.

> If we're going to have media for vibrant democratic culture, we have to plan for it, try it out, show people that it matters, and build new constituencies to invest in it. . . . The first and crucial step is to embrace the participatory – the feature that has also been most dis-ruptive of current media models. We also need standards and metrics to define truly meaningful participation in media for public life. And we need policies, initiatives, and sustainable financial models that can turn today's assets and experiments into tomorrow's tried-and-true public media. (Clark & Aufderheide 2009)

It is difficult, however, to define exactly what constitutes mean-ingful participation. Mike Ananny and Kate Hennessy (2008), in reference to the future of museums and the press, write, "To cri-tique the idea that participation is always just, always educational, and always empowering does not mean rejecting the emancipatory potential of emerging technologies. Rather, such a critical perspec-tive can salvage the idea of participation, protecting it from being narcotized by celebratory rhetoric." Jodi Dean (2008) describes what she calls the fantasy of participation, where people falsely

148

believe that their input – a comment, a signature on an online survey, linking to other content – is contributing to the information stream, a sort of communicative action. "Weirdly, then," she writes, "the circulation of communication is depoliticizing, not because people don't care or don't want to be involved, but because we do! Or put more precisely, it is depoliticizing because the form of our involvement ultimately empowers those it is supposed to resist" (2008: 110). Former *Newsweek* reporter Eric Pape echoes this when he says: "I'm all for the masses sharing in the debate and in contributing when it is meaningful, the problem is that, so often, it isn't particularly meaningful and it is really just about giving the masses the impression that half-formed comment-rants are valued. (In fact, they are. They help smart online sites to sell ads)" (unpublished correspondence with author 2010). A better news environment that places networked publics at the center and that extends participation beyond the fantasy Dean describes will see more energy and resources concentrated on digital literacy.

Henry Jenkins (2006) explains that emergent illiteracies concern individual expression less and community involvement more. "The new literacies almost all involve social skills developed through collaboration and networking. These skills build on the foundation of traditional literacy, research skills, technical skills, and critical analysis skills taught in the classroom." He suggests a certain set of fundamental skills associated with new literacies, including appropriation or the ability to sample and remix media content; multitasking or the ability to scan and shift attention as needed to salient details; collective intelligence or the ability to pool knowledge and compare notes with others toward a common goal; and judgment or the ability to evaluate the reliability and credibility of different information sources, among others. Ultimately, however, digital literacy is not about learning a universal set of skills but rather about developing an understanding of a new set of social practices and meaning making mediated by digital texts (Lankshear & Knobels 2008).

While Jenkins' report focuses on youth and digital literacy, there are a number of examples of successful efforts aimed at fostering digital literacy among adults in order to increase the quality and diversity of participation. The Denver Open Media Foundation (OMF) provides new media and video training workshops, loans out equipment, and has designed an open-source platform that automates programming for three public-access stations. The viewer community votes for its favorite shows, which then move into the most highly trafficked timeslots on air. In 2007, the OMF won a Knight News Challenge Grant to develop its open-source tools for use at public-access television stations, community technology centers, and other noncommercial community media projects across the country and to encourage greater community engagement at those projects. Essentially, the OMF is helping public-access stations battered by public funding cuts to survive by updating their organizational structures and their publishing tools. The goal is to create a larger network for sharing content among stations, a sort of public access YouTube that operates more effectively and democratically than the stand-alone stations do now, to further engage community participants. Similarly, the international human rights organization Witness is now partnering with human rights groups around the world to train and support them in working video into their methods and missions to increase visibility and impact. In 2010 Witness launched WitnessHub, a public platform aimed at forging relationships among organizations and participant networks and creating a broader, more interconnected global human rights community.

The value of these innovative projects is that they work to improve participation rather than uncritically celebrating all participation. Witness shapes the communication environment by encouraging certain types and styles of content through training and support. The OMF provides tools and training to promote community engagement as its main product; the Foundation itself is agnostic where content is concerned. These models of innovation around participation, however, depend in large part on increasingly equal public access to digital information, which includes the extension of so-called "net neutrality," and they also underline the way efforts to extend participation as a most highly prized asset in the networked era butt up against current intellectual property law.

Net Neutrality

The movement for net neutrality is a response to the growing power of telephone and cable network operators (TCNO) over internet access in the broadband era. The current "end-to-end" design, in which all content, platforms, and sites are treated equally, was protected until 2005, when the Federal Communications Commission eliminated the rules that prohibited cable and phone companies from discriminating against content providers. The communications companies have argued that building and maintaining state-of-the-art networks and increasing access to those networks will cost money, which they can raise by providing preferential treatment in the form of tiered better services for those willing and able to pay and worse or no services for those unwilling and unable to pay. That sounds reasonable from a business perspective but it would re-create the limited information environment of the mass-media era, where everyone may have had access to the airwaves but for most of the last fifty years there were only five channels for anyone to watch with shows produced by an extremely limited number of people – a deeply unsatisfying media environment compared to the one produced in the equal-access internet age. Laurence Lessig and Robert McChesney (2006) in a *Washington Post* op-ed explained it this way:

> [The cable and phone companies] would be able to sell access to the express lane to deep-pocketed corporations and relegate everyone else to the digital equivalent of a winding dirt road. Worse still, these gatekeepers would determine who gets premium treatment and who doesn't. Their idea is to stand between the content provider and the consumer, demanding a toll to guarantee quality delivery.

Supporters of net neutrality, including Tim Berners-Lee, inventor of the World Wide Web, argue that innovation depends on the preservation of a neutral network and advocate the establishment of a legal mandate ensuring that communications companies are not allowed to act as gatekeepers. In the absence of the neutral network, momentum building toward democratic participation would be buried:

We would lose the opportunity to vastly expand access and distribution of independent news and community information through broadband television. More than 60 percent of Web content is created by regular people, not corporations. How will this innovation and production thrive if creators must seek permission from a cartel of network owners? (Lessig & McChesney 2006)

The appointment of outspoken proponent of net neutrality Julius Genachowski as chairman of the Federal Communications Commission raised hopes for net neutrality supporters, but because of the limited powers of the FCC to regulate the internet, the principle has been dealt a series of blows in the federal court. Yet even if the FCC wins authority to guard equal access, there is no guarantee that it will secure net neutrality. The Electronic Frontier Foundation points out the FCC has a history of privileging the commercial and special interest over grassroots public opinion. There is already concern over the FCC's promise to make an exception to net neutrality for the purpose of copyright enforcement (McSherry 2009). In the words of Electronic Frontier Foundation Civil Liberties Director Jennifer Granick: "We already see corporate lobbyists and 'public decency' advocates pushing for loopholes [in net neutrality laws]. . . . ISPs will claim copyright enforcement as a pretext for all sorts of discriminatory behavior" (Anderson 2010).

Copyright Reform

The issue of copyright enforcement, like that of net neutrality, is shaping the future of digital communications. Media outlets are exploring ways to put up paywalls and track down content to prevent its free dissemination. The Press+ (http://www.journal-ismonline.com/index.html), which claims to be "pioneering the effort to make the transition to a paid online," maintains that hundreds of daily and weekly newspapers have signed letters of intent to explore its tools that will force readers to buy news from a single pass-protected site. Another development company, Attributor (http://www.attributor.com/), is creating tools to "fingerprint" digital content so it can be tracked and billed for all over the web. AP recently announced its plans to track and seek payment for its products. Yet one of the most common ways people engage with news is by sharing and discussing it within their social networks. In spirit and practice, erecting paywalls and criminalizing the spread of content hobble the greatest, most inherent feature of the digital communications network.

Laurence Lessig (2008) argues that with the shift from a Read Only culture, where our relationship to cultural products is limited to that of passive consumers, to Read Write culture, where our relationship to cultural products is characterized by engagement with the material, where we remix, comment on, tag, aggregate, there is an urgent need to reconsider laws protecting intellectual property. He argues that "the extreme regulation that copyright law has become makes it difficult, and sometimes impossible, for a wide range of creativity that any free society – if it thought about it for just a second – would allow to exist, legally" (Lessig 2008: 18). The criminalizing of creativity, Lessig argues, has corrupted a whole generation of young people, "those who do what technology encourages them to do" (2008: xix).

Increasingly, journalists, artists, and other content creators are attaching to their work Creative Commons licenses, an alternative to the "all rights reserved" of traditional copyright. Creative Commons, a non-profit founded by Lessig and other reform advocates, is devoted to increasing the number and range of works available for people to build on and share legally. The organization makes available copyright licenses that allow creators to communicate which rights they reserve and which rights they wave. Journalists may attach a license to their work that gives permissions for the work to be shared freely but not for a profit.[1] In 2006 GateHouse Media, which owns 75 dailies and 231 weeklies in the U.S., adopted Creative Commons licenses for content of most of its outlets, which was most likely an effort to encourage bloggers and other web publishers to quote stories at length, driving traffic back to the newspaper and increasing its Google ranking and increasing ad revenue (Williams 2006). Indeed, many independent and commercial journalistic endeavors are using Creative Commons licenses, including the *New York Times* and Al Jazeera. Many more are using photos and other Creative Commons content they find on sharing sites. To help people find content that is free to use, Creative Commons runs a search engine that searches only for CC licensed materials.

The success of efforts like that of CC and those working to protect net neutrality are essential to building a networked news landscape that supports active publics. But the result of these efforts is far from certain. So far, the networked era has produced more outspoken, critical, and mobilized publics but news organizations remain largely tied to structures of ownership, authority, and professionalism that at their core clash with new modes of participation and sources of authority.

In journalism and across cultural industry sectors, the people formerly known as news consumers are now integral to the process of production and distribution. In the ways that they participate in creating and circulating news, networked publics have already crossed countless hurdles to profoundly influence traditional journalism institutions and products. The diversity introduced over the past decade has energized the field of journalism even as it has rocked the news industry business model and wreaked havoc with journalism as a paying profession. As Washington Independent editor Aaron Weiner (2010) wrote on the day his three-year-old nonprofit politics news site shuttered in November 2010, "the crisis in the world of journalism today isn't really about journalism – it's about the bottom line." Weiner's colleague, Colorado *Independent* editor John Tomasic, said the defunct Washington Independent, an all-online outlet, is a revealing artifact of the "great transition."

> The journalism was solid by all the standard measures and by most of what you might call new journalism standards too. The Washington Independent was lean and fast and concerned with complicated policy. It placed accountability at the top of its priorities and it raised transparency above objectivity. It was also very popular with readers. The problem was only money. I say only money because Americans are good at making money and they will find a way to turn all of this energy and public interest in journalism product into profits. It's just

a matter of time. Question is, Will the new media profit-makers leave it at "only money" or will they fundamentally change the spirit of the new refreshing product in the process and for the worse? (Unpublished interview with author 2010)

Although there are still wide swaths of the population that don't have access to high-speed internet, the ranks of contributors to contemporary news content in its broadest sense are still swelling and they are at least formally free from the homogenizing influence of professionalism. The new forms of journalism characterizing the "great transition" are empowering a more diverse cross-section of people to communicate in ways that they see fit, to develop new genres and styles as part of their participation, and they are expanding conversation as a result. The content of that participation has often been judged harshly, but the effect of participation has included greater critical awareness about authority in general and journalism in particular, an undeniably positive development in a democracy and arguably one of the main objectives of the best journalism of the mass-media professional news era. Truth as the exclusive domain of authorities and the journalists who use them as sources has been receding and making way for communication created by the public based on storytelling, exchange, and perspectives that have been traditionally excluded. In the face of eroding civil rights, increased media concentration, and intense public mistrust of government and media, this struggle is integrally tied to the struggle for the revival of public life and the role of public discourse in democracy.

Note

1 For a complete list of the licenses available and a more thorough account of Creative Commons, see http://www.creativecommons.org.

References

American Society of News Editors (2009) "U.S. Newsroom Employment Declines." April 16. http://asne.org/article_view/smid/370/articleid/12/reftab/101.aspx

Anderson, B. (1983) *Imagined Communities: Reflections on the Origin and Spread of Nationalism*. New York: Verso.

Ananny, M. & Hennessy, K. (2008) "The Future of Public Institutions: New Media, The Press & The Museum." Report on symposium held May 2–3, 2008 at the University of British Columbia.

Anderson, N. (2010) "EFF Demands FCC Close Copyright 'Loophole' in Net Neutrality." Arstechnica. http://arstechnica.com/tech-policy/news/2010/03/eff-demands-fcc-close-copyright-loophole-in-net-neutrality.ars

Carey, J. (1989) *Communication as Culture*. Boston: Unwin Hyman.

Clark, J. & Aufderheide, P. (2009) "Public Media 2.0: Dynamic Engaged Publics." Center For Social Media Report. http://www.centerfor socialmedia.org/resources/publications/public_media_2_0_dynamic_engaged_publics/

Dean, J. (2008) "Communicative Capitalism: Circulation and Foreclosure of Politics." In: M. Boler (ed.), *Digital Media and Democracy: Tactics in Hard Times*. Cambridge, MA: MIT Press.

Deuze, M. (2007) *Media Work*. Cambridge: Polity.

Dickinson, E. (2011) "The First WikiLeaks Revolution?" ForeignPolicy.com, January 3. http://wikileaks.foreignpolicy.com/posts/2011/01/13/wikileaks_and_the_tunisia_protests?sms_ss=twitter&at_xt=4d2ffe4d9c2649d7,1

Gitidharadas, A. (2010) "Africa's Gift to Silicon Valley: How to Track a Crisis." *New York Times*, March 14. http://www.nytimes.com/2010/03/14/weekinreview/14giridharadas.html

Glaser, M. (2004) "'Nerd Values' Help Propel Tiny Craigslist into Classifieds Threat." Online Journalism Review. http://www.ojr.org/ojr/business/1086222946.php

Glasser, T. (2000) "Play and the Power of News." *Journalism: Theory, Practice and Criticism* 1, 23–9.

Greenwald, G. (2010a) "The War on WikiLeaks and Why It Matters." Salon.com, March 27. http://www.salon.com/news/opinion/glenn_greenwald/2010/03.27/wikileaks

Greenwald, G. (2010b) "The Strange and Consequential Case of Bradley Manning, Adrian Lamo and WikiLeaks." Salon.com, June 18. http://www.salon.com/news/opinion/glenn_greenwald/2010/06/18/wikileaks

Hartley, J. (2008) "Journalism as a Human Right: The Cultural Approach to Journalism." In: M. Loffelholz & D. Weaver (eds), *Global Journalism Research*. New York: Wiley-Blackwell.

Jenkins, H. (2006). "Confronting the Challenges of Participatory Culture: Media Education of the 21st Century." National Writing Project Report. http://www.nwp.org/cs/public/print/resource/2713

Lankshear, C. & Knobels, M. (2008) *Digital Literacies: Concepts, Policies, and Practices*. New York: Peter Lang.

Leonard, T. (2010) "Pentagon Deems WikiLeaks a National Security Threat."

Telegraph, March 18. http://www.telegraph.co.uk/technology/7475050/
Pentagon-deems-Wikileaks-a-national-security-threat.html

Lessig, L. (2008) *Remix*. New York: Penguin Press.

Lessig, L. & McChesney, R. (2006) "No Tolls on the Internet." *Washington Post*,
June 8. http://www.washingtonpost.com/wp-dyn/content/article/2006/06/07/
AR2006060702108.html

McChesney, R. & Nichols, J. (2009) "The Death and Life of the Great
American Newspaper." *The Nation*, March 18. http://www.thenation.com/
doc/20090406/nichols_mcchesney/

McChesney, R. & Nichols, J. (2010) *The Death and Life of American Journalism*.
New York: Nation Books.

McSherry, C. (2009) "Is Net Neutrality a FCC Trojan Horse?" EFF, October 21.
http://www.eff.org/deeplinks/2009/09/net-neutrality-fcc-perils-and-promise

Pew (2010) "The State of the News Media: An Annual Report on American
Journalism." Pew Project for Excellence in Journalism. http://www.stateofthe-
media.org/2010/overview_key_findings.php

Purcell, K., Rainie, L., Mitchell, A., Rosenstiel, T. & Olmstead, K. (2010).
"Understanding the Participatory News Consumer." Pew Internet and
American Life Project, March 1. http://www.pewinternet.org/Reports/2010/
Online-News.aspx

Putnam, R (2000) *Bowling Alone*. New York: Simon & Schuster.

Rosen, J. (2006) "The People Formerly Known as the Audience." PressThink,
June 27. http://journalism.nyu.edu/pubzone/weblogs/pressthink/2006/06/27/
ppl_frmr.html

Rosen, J. (2009) Session on Social Media. Knight Center for Specialized
Journalism Conference. Posted December 7. http://www.youtube.com/
watch?v=2zqK9T9Sneo

Schudson, M. (2003) *The Sociology of News*. New York: W.W. Norton.

Schudson, M. & Downie, Jr., L. (2009) "The Reconstruction of American
Journalism." *Columbia Journalism Review*, October 19. http://www.cjr.org/
reconstruction/the_reconstruction_of_american.php

Shirky, C. (2009) "Newspapers and Thinking the Unthinkable." http://www.
shirky.com/weblog/2009/03/newspapers-and-thinking-the-unthinkable/

Sunstein, C. (2002) *Republic.com*. Princeton, N.J.: Princeton University Press.

Van Buskirk, E. (2010) "Snowmageddon Site Crowdsources Blizzard Cleanup."
February 10. http://www.wired.com/epicenter/2010/02/snowmageddon-
crowdsources-blizzard-clean-up/

Walker, P. (2010) "Julian Assange: WikiLeaks Faces 'Very Aggressive'
Investigation by US." *Guardian*, December 17. http://www.guardian.co.uk/
media/2010/dec/17/julian-assange-wikileaks-us-investigation

Weiner, A. (2010) "Washington Independent, Signing Off." Washington
Independent, November 17. http://washingtonindependent.com/103701/the-
washington-independent-signing-off

Wesch, M. (2008) "An Anthropological Introduction to YouTube." Video of Library of Congress presentation. http://mediatedcultures.net/ksudigg/?p=179

Williams, L. (2006) "Newspaper Chain Goes Creative Commons: GateHouse Media Rolls CC Over 96 Newspaper Sites." PressThink, December 15. http://journalism.nyu.edu/pubzone/weblogs/pressthink/2006/12/15/newspaper_chain.html

Index

Index

Index

Index

Index

Index

Index

Index

Index